ADVENTURES OF A SERIAL
ENTREPRENEUR

Fortunes made, lost and made again

ADVENTURES OF A SERIAL ENTREPRENEUR

Achievements over Adversity

FRED DUFFY

Published in 2020 by

Court Books, Dublin, Ireland

Copyright © 2020 Fred Duffy

The right of Fred Duffy to be identified as the author of this book has been
asserted in accordance with the Copyright, Designs and Patents Act, 1988

ISBN (paperback) 978-1-8382650-0-7

ISBN (ebook) 978-1-8382650-1-4

Cover Design and Interior Layout by designforwriters.com

To

Helen, my wonderful wife, friend and mentor without
whose support many of these events wouldn't have
happened, and this chronicle would never have been
finished

and

my four children and their four partners:
exciting, adventurous, entrepreneurial,
a challenging cohort of love, joy and laughter

CONTENTS

INTRODUCTION

THIS BIOGRAPHY WAS STARTED in response to repeated suggestions from my family that I should record the numerous stories they had heard over the years. This statement, by my daughter Sinead, says it all: 'As Dad sat down to every dinnertime with stories of the lows and highs that happened on a very regular basis, the joy he had must have been contagious – the joy of creating something that might make a difference in people's lives and might just go the distance.'

It is not a conventional biography, but more an adventure story arising out of an entrepreneur's ventures which sometimes lead to unexpected – and mostly unwarranted – situations.

In writing about the mishaps that occasionally interrupted my life, I found I was reliving them. Together, they intruded on an otherwise normal and enjoyable career. Anecdotes of danger, of fortunes made, lost and remade; of competitive spying; death threats; detention by Merseyside police; misadventure; confronting a Saudi army commander; award of the year for business enterprise... the list goes on. I'm hoping that these extraordinary and sometimes dramatic incidents may be of interest.

Writing this biography has had a profound effect on me. It has made me realize that my life is the story of a serial entrepreneur. If I had remained working in a safe secure job in Irish Shell, most of these events wouldn't have occurred and you wouldn't be reading this book.

The strange thing was to discover that at a time when I should be retired, I am still driven by the passion to create – in this case, stories which I simply need to write and which hopefully may engage some readers.

At an age when I should be spending my time on Sudoku, I have been waylaid by my own adage:

When you have lived your dreams
you cannot go back to sleeping.

I will confine my writing to non-fiction, and hope to publish four books over the next twelve months.

This is the first one and I do hope you enjoy it.

Fred Duffy
Dublin, Autumn 2020

CHAPTER 1:
EARLY DAYS IN MONAGHAN

DING-DING: AS THE SOFT bell sounded, I looked up from my paper at the discreet interruption. The softly-spoken voice of the Eurostar conductor announced: 'Mesdames et Messieurs, the train has now reached 300 km/h, we will arrive in the Gare du Nord in fifty-five minutes.'

At 186 mph, I looked at my coffee cup: not a tremor – no indication of our speed. We were bringing our son Michael to Paris for lunch to celebrate his safe arrival home from his gap year in Southeast Asia. As the sleek Pininfarina-designed train streaked through the Normandy countryside I thought, St Pancras to Paris in little more than two hours. How far we had come…

Monaghan is a small town just south of the border with Northern Ireland. Designed by the settlers who came over with the Ulster plantation, it has a neat layout with a central diamond rather than a square. My family owned a shop in the Diamond, which meant we were party to any excitement. Born in 1933, that first decade was an interesting time for me. Although it was a county town, it really had a village style and atmosphere. We had pleasant relationships with most of our neighbours; they bought from us and we bought from them.

It was a very safe environment for a child growing up, and though my options were limited, there was lots of excitement and wonder for all that. Life moved at a slower pace in those days. We walked or cycled, we took time to observe, to participate and to enjoy situations unfolding all around us. There was no TV, papers were scarce enough, and Radio Éireann had a limited repertoire so people depended more on the spoken word – often inaccurate – and on gossip. But it meant that people had time for each other. There were few telephones and we wrote letters, unless urgent – in which case we sent a telegram.

This all meant that the little boy in the centre of Monaghan could enjoy his busy, busy world, and there was such a world of activities and adventures to see. The blacksmith's forge was one of the main attractions, where the smithy used to let me work the arm of the bellows. Located in the Market Yard, it was a huge, black cavern of a place, with nervous horses and the blacksmith heating the shoes and hammering them into shape. The drama came alive when the smithy approached the horse with a red-hot horseshoe: the horse panics, rearing onto its back legs as the farmer holds onto the bridle. With the confidence of long experience, the smithy grabs the horse's hoof, holds it between his legs and presses the hot shoe onto the hissing hoof with a cloud of smoke and the smell of burned bone. What a show! We'd only have time to see one or we'd be late for our lessons.

When I was sent on messages I was accepted into the workings of all sorts of exciting places, like the shoemaker in Dublin Street. Mr Montague was a very nice man and I spent many an hour in his workroom. He worked alone, and maybe he was glad of the company. I loved the smell of the leather and polish and the whirr of the foot-driven polishing machine.

McGills, our next-door neighbours, were watchmakers. Old Mr McGill was a tiny white-haired man, who I never saw without his watchmaker's glass stuck in his eye like a monocle. His sons, Gerry and Seamus, were both expert watchmakers and, more importantly, model-makers. They filled their windows with Wellington and Lancaster bombers fighting with Stukkers and Messerschmitts.

A message to go to Sherry's Bakery would bring me the length of Dublin Street, past several places at which to stop and stare. Gillander's, the butchers, killed cattle at the back of the premises – happily far enough and down the entry for us not to be too aware of it. Old Mr Gillander was big and looked strong as an ox. The sons were also big, but the old man had the advantage of more years of eating good beef. The entire shopfront consisted of removable planks so that the shop was totally open to the footpath, with a number of huge carcasses hanging from hooks and the floor covered with sawdust fresh every morning. There was always something happening.

McCoy's bicycle shop was always busy and I wasn't allowed into the workshop, but I could look from the door.

Sherry's Bakery had a huge coke-fired oven and I would go as close as the heat on my face allowed. I can still taste the fresh bread.

Graham's bacon factory, in the corner of the Diamond, was inspected regularly by the government veterinary inspector, Larry McIlhargey, a good friend of the family, a good customer and very popular with me and my brothers. He gave us an exclusive supply of the pig's bladder for footballs, which give us a magical barter opportunity.

Another regular adventure was my journey to the local creamery to collect a quart of cream every Saturday. This brought us past Patton's Yard, with its corn mills, timber and hardware; a hive of activity and a hub of adventure. We could get free rides by hanging on to the back of the horse-drawn lorries or flats. We filled our pockets with handfuls of yellow corn in the hope of eating it – which of course we couldn't.

A definite advantage of living in the shop was the amount of town intelligence we got and passed on. With many people popping in for the paper and cigarettes, we received and reported all the gossip of the day. Gossip in a small town left few secrets. For example, one leading businessman was well known to have more than an eye for the ladies and when his marriage led to divorce – almost unknown at the time – it caused a sensation. The sale of the *News of the World* was prohibited in Ireland, but suddenly hundreds of copies started arriving in the post as we all followed the sordid details. The story kept us gossiping for weeks.

There was one Sunday morning when our customers coming from the twelve o'clock Mass couldn't get into a shop fast enough, then they wouldn't leave, and the shop was packed with excited Mass-goers. Apparently, our neurotic Bishop had really gone too far. From the pulpit, he had denounced the local golf club as a Protestant den of debauchery and drunkenness. I think he went on to forbid Catholics from frequenting it in the future.

Every town had a local drunk and we had a very colourful character. A vagrant alcoholic, he wore a jaunty hat, scruffy clothes and usually talked loudly to himself. On his good days he would try to sell penny song-sheets and would occasionally put his hat on the ground and sing unintelligibly in the hope of getting a few pence. Many times, I saw him pass out on the ground drunk, and sometimes – often on a Fair Day – I watched him in terror as he fought, bloodied and rather stupidly, with other drunks.

Two spinster ladies owned a pub halfway down Dublin Street and had a pet turkey, Harry, who was treated and regarded as one of the family. They were not well-off, and one Christmas they thought they would like to have turkey for the Christmas dinner. They couldn't afford to buy one, so Harry would have to go. They kept putting off the actual killing but decided to pluck the bird in preparation. When it came to the bit, however, they found they couldn't kill him, and Harry was spared. The next question was whether Harry could survive the winter cold with no feathers. Solution: they knitted him a cardigan and pair of pants which kept him warm. Harry became a familiar figure strutting up Dublin Street in his knitted outfit, causing many visiting motorists to swear off drink.

A man living further down the road, Peter McDonald, raised chickens and learned how to whistle to them so that they would follow him up and down his yard – Monaghan's own chicken whisperer.

Once every month we had the Monaghan Fair which was held in Park Street, although we had a large Market Yard. It was a treat for me walking home from school to pick my way through flocks of chickens and geese, pigs, calves and cattle. We could watch the farmers and dealers wheeling and playacting until a deal was done; one would spit on his hand and give a high-five to the other, at which stage they would usually repair to the nearest pub for a pint. You wouldn't see a better show at the Puskar Camel fair in India or in Marrakesh. The mess on the streets was pretty dreadful but by nightfall, council workers had swept and hosed the place down.

Cassidy's bus was painted yellow and brown and had neither name nor any destination shown. It didn't need either, as everyone knew that it only travelled between Monaghan and Scotstown. Its colour distinguished it from all other buses in my world, which were blue and yellow with letters GNR (Great Northern Railways) along both sides. It was many years later that I descended from the train at Amiens Street station in

Dublin to discover with some shock that every bus in sight was green and some had two storeys.

Cassidy's Bus started every day in Scotstown, the village where my mother had grown up. Margaret Caulfield was born on 3 September 1897. Her grandfather was Henry Caulfield who wore a top hat and owned a flax mill, probably in Omagh. Neither my American cousins nor I have been able to trace the lineage of the Caulfields. Scotstown is close to the Northern Ireland border, which had been hurriedly drawn through rough mountain terrain with no main roads, ideal for smuggling and IRA covert activities.

Two of her brothers, Brian and Frank, were members of the old IRA and engaged in active service against the British forces. On one occasion when the men were resting at home, a truckload of the dreaded Black and Tans pulled up on the road and a troop of armed men ran up the sloping lane towards the house. Margaret ran to the front and with a broad smile on her face got ready to chat up the soldiers to give her brothers time to escape. It didn't work. Soldiers ran through the house chasing her brothers, shots were fired but they were out of range, running for their lives. Later, Brian paid a heavy price for his bravery when he took a bullet in the leg and was jailed in England.

These were bad days for Ireland. The British were incensed by the 1916 revolution. They handled a sensitive situation with such clumsiness as to turn the entire population against them. They made two historically stupid decisions. Firstly, they executed all the captured leaders of the revolution. This was protracted over several weeks, and included shooting the Trade Union leader, James Connelly, who had been so badly wounded, they had to tie him to a chair to shoot him sitting down. The public felt that the revolutionaries should have been tried as prisoners of war and not criminals. Compounding their clumsiness, the British assembled a militia to discipline the Irish. Few professional soldiers could be freed from the war effort so they selected volunteers from the dregs of the British population: layabouts and jailbirds released from prison with a mandate to shake the Irish up a bit, keeping any booty taken. Dressed in non-descript black and brown uniforms, they were soon known as the Black and Tans. History has recorded their brutal destruction throughout Ireland, which stiffened the resolve of the population, leading to the Free State.

My mother Margaret became a runner for the IRA and carried communications, cycling through the Black and Tan roadblocks, as any innocent girl would. At that time, her doctor was the village doctor, Leo Reynolds. It is just possible that he treated my uncle Brian for the gunshot wound. One day, the Black and Tans drove a truck through the village with Dr Reynolds standing on the rear, a gun to his head: 'Reveal your IRA supporters or we'll shoot the doctor.' Nobody flinched, and the doctor was brought off to the Crumlin Road jail in Belfast. At the same time his brother, Dr Joe Reynolds, served with the British troops in France. He was awarded a medal to be decorated at Buckingham Palace but refused to accept it. He explained, 'My brother was only doing what I was doing – attending to wounded men, but you have put him in jail.' Many years later, it turned out that those brothers were my wife's uncles. Joe Reynolds entertained us to dinner in the Royal Marine hotel in Dun Laoghaire. It was many years later that his daughter Moira discovered his medal hidden in a drawer.

In spite of the Black and Tans, life was good in Scotstown and when the First World War ended, Margaret got a job as a schoolteacher and enjoyed seaside holidays with her cousins, the Carrols. She was, no doubt, pleased to greet her sister Rose on holidays back from New York with her husband Fred Duffy. On several occasions, she enjoyed the company of Fred's brother

Joseph, a good-looking building contractor with apparently sufficient means to offer her a good future. Although there was a considerable age difference, thirty-eight to twenty-five, they married in 1922. My father's interests were wide ranging: politics, world affairs, collecting antiques, demolition of buildings. He was very ethical, sensitive and romantic but not very streetwise. As little as my mother knew about the retail business, he knew less; yet my mother converted one of the buildings inherited from Joe's father into a small shop. Highly focused, she had the drive and initiative to follow her ambitions and their business soon outgrew the small shop. Besides, the children kept coming: there were now four, and she needed more space. When a large retail shop became vacant in the prestigious Diamond in the centre of the town, she pressed Joseph to secure the tenancy from Lord Rossmore, the ground landlord. The shop soon was to become known as 'Duffy's of the Diamond'. It was a bold initiative for poor upstart Catholics to start a shop in the main square of a very Protestant border town. There were Harper's, Crawford's, Patton's, McCaldin's, Gillander's, Henry's, Royal Bank, Ulster Bank, the Westenra Hotel; potentially challenging neighbours.

By the time I began to take an interest, her father had given up contracting and had positioned himself as one of the town elders. He was on the Town Council and the County Council and a founder member of the Fianna Fáil party. De Valera realised that he needed a newspaper for propaganda purposes and founded the Irish Press as his voice against the *Irish Times* and the Fine Gael-supporting *Irish Independent*. My father subscribed for ten one pound-shares in September 1929. Viewed from a purely local perspective, De Valera can readily be criticised in the context of the Civil War and the painful birth pangs of a fledgling nation, as well as for his economic war with Britain which was clearly ill-judged. Looking at this from a global view, however, I believe he was the right man to hold Ireland together in a turbulent world that was tearing itself apart; a world where a small defenceless country in a strategically important location could easily fall to one of the great powers. I believe that we owe much to this man who, under great pressure, demonstrated strong, level-headed leadership that won him and Ireland the respect of world powers.

Cassidy's daily bus service brought commuters and school-children the five miles to Monaghan where it turned around in the Market Yard and parked in its usual spot in Park Street, facing out towards Scotstown, until it left again at about midday. It repeated this journey in the afternoon, and every day of the week except Sunday. I walked past it on my way to and from school, a centre of activity; farmers' wives clutching chickens, newspapers being loaded, bags of mail and on a Fair Day, a number of tipsy farmers, persuaded it was time to go home, that 'the tea would be ready'. Once a year, I would travel on it with my crammed suitcase for my annual holidays.

Uncle Frank was a farmer and had a large family of cousins for me to play with. Scotstown became a magical place for me where I could leave my shoes in the bedroom and walk barefoot on the tarmac road. It was where my bigger cousins would show me the constellations of stars in the night sky – no light pollution there; where I could learn to swim aged eight; where every Friday we ran down to meet the bakers van and get a free bun.

Life on a farm in the 1930s and 1940s was pretty basic. I slept in the large boys' room on a straw mattress on the floor. There was no electric light and illumination at night was from one paraffin lamp. There was linoleum in the parlour, which never seemed to be used; the rest of the floor was flagstones.

Cooking was done on an open turf fire which provided the only heat in the house. It was all done in cast-iron pots hanging from hooks or sitting in the hot embers, sometimes with turf on top of the pot. These three-legged pots were used for boiling potatoes and the flat cast iron ovens produced flat cakes of soda bread. I churned butter and enjoyed it unsalted, on the warm, freshly-baked bread, with a spread of apple jam just made in a tin cup. Delicious.

The main meal was at midday but if the men were working in the far fields or on the bog we brought them baskets of thickly-buttered, freshly-baked bread, and tea so strong you could walk on it. We had freshly-dug smiling potatoes, fresh butter and buttermilk. On Sunday Auntie Kathleen killed a chicken, or if times were good, we had roast beef.

Toilet facilities were non-existent, one went into the woods to defecate. Dock leaves were good for wiping your bum (not like that in the town where we had newspaper – there was a war on). The three-legged pot boiled the water to sterilise the milk churns which were filled each morning, then left on the roadside for collection by the creamery lorry en route to Monaghan creamery.

There was a ceilidh in the kitchen one evening, a fiddle player and a melodeon player providing the music; the neighbours came in and everyone danced, including this little townie.

Once a week, Cassidy's bus would stop at the bottom of our street, the honk of the horn announcing a parcel of sweets from mum, sweets to be shared with all the cousins.

My mother's brother, Uncle Frank, was a dark, taciturn man who hardly spoke, while Auntie Kathleen was full of life. She taught me the best places to look for the free-range eggs and how to catch a chicken for the Sunday lunch. And when she cut off its head, the chicken would simply run around the yard before dropping to the ground. Of course, I wanted to help milk the cows, but I couldn't get a drop into the bucket while my older cousins could squirt me with milk at six feet.

One Sunday, Master Murray arrived in a motorcar. Wearing a hat and his Sunday best, he was calling on my older cousin Rose, a fine-looking woman of about twenty-five. The car was a temptation and when we released the handbrake, we hadn't allowed for the slope down the street to the man road. Somehow, we stopped it and Master Murray didn't make it an issue.

Sunday was special as Uncle Frank, big cousins Charlie and Matt polished the trap, backed in the horse and we all piled in to it, off to Mass in our finest. Uncle Frank wore a bowler hat. Another special memory was saving the hay and piling it into the barn. Summers were sunnier in Scotstown.

There was no cinema in the village, so it was a special event when the touring theatre came for two weeks of live drama. A canvas marquee was erected to hold about a hundred and twenty people on hard benches, with a generator lighting the interior. In a village with no electricity, this was an event in itself and the coloured lights at the entrance seemed to brighten the entire village. The repertoire included *Gypsy*, *The Rose of Killarney*, and, best of all, *Maria and the Red Barn*. To describe the performances as melodramatic doesn't do justice to the overacting, which galvanised the audience into active support with groans for the victims and hisses for the villains. Modern cinema doesn't arouse the same emotions.

Back at school, things were boring so I was surprised in our second week in second class when we were paraded out to a field in the Armagh Road, where we were given an hour's exercise running and playing. We were told to bring football boots every Wednesday, which would be concentrated on football. What a surprise, what a treat; this would challenge our marbles and hoops.

Another discovery that year was the school outing. The railway journey to Glaslough was only five miles, but it was exciting. Our outing was to Castle Leslie, the home of Sir Shane Leslie. He personally welcomed us and showed us all over the house which was a museum of collectables with special reference to his cousin Winston Churchill. It rained all day, and the sandwiches got soaked, but it was a great outing which I still remember with nostalgia.

Our location in the centre of the town had many advantages, as the Diamond ground was concrete and many of the key games worked best on concrete: spinning tops, roller-skating, rolling hoops, playing marbles, tricycles and later bicycles. There was no end of games to play or neighbours to play them with.

Living in a shop likewise had many advantages. Because we sold marbles and hoops, roller skates and spinning tops and many such novelties, we usually had a steady supply for ourselves. If there was something we didn't have, we'd swap a few pigs bladders, maybe, for a bigger marble or a champion chestnut. We sold elastic by the foot for repairing the elastic in ladies' underwear, but it worked very well with a suitable sapling to make a bow and arrow for cowboys and Indians.

Halloween was an exciting introduction to the approaching winter with nights closing in, bright lights and cosy fires. Long before the American influence introduced large pumpkin heads and Trick or Treat, we had enjoyed traditional Irish games from times past. We had no fireworks but didn't miss them as we made our own bangers. Calcium carbide was widely used to light bicycle lamps, and we were all familiar with it. The effect of water on the carbide was to produce acetylene gas, highly combustible. We could put some into a tin can with a tight, but not screwed, lid. When darkness fell, we could place it outside a target hall door, add water, and run. In about two minutes the expanding gas would blow the lid off with a highly satisfying bang. The best thing was that the victim couldn't see what had caused the bang as the tin had blown away. We could recover it later and use it again and again until all the carbide had been used. Nasty little boys, perhaps, but great fun.

I have many happy memories of Christmas when I was young. My father made a big fuss of the event and personally picked the Christmas tree, usually a big one. This was lit by live wax candles, the sort still used on birthday cakes; a real fire risk, with hindsight. One year he donned a Santa Claus outfit but when he was seen coming down the stairs dressed up, the maid screamed and ran to hide in the kitchen, which frightened us children and we all started crying. He didn't wear it again. Cowboys and Indian outfits were serious toys in those days, along with guns and lead soldiers. We had a big toy section in a local shop and it was a real challenge for my mother and the shop girls to keep our hands from prying.

I wasn't allowed to go to the pictures until I was ten so it was a great excitement when we learned that the Maclin boys were going to put on a small private film show; I could come if I paid a penny and if I kept quiet. This film starred Charlie Chaplin. We all assembled in Maclin's pig yard for the big occasion – the Maclins were pig dealers and had a number of pigsties up the back of the yard. These sties were always hosed down, swept and kept very clean, which was helpful because that is where the film show would take place. Planks were placed from the sides of the pens to form seats.

Light was a problem, too much of it, so someone was dispatched to place sacks over the roof lights. This all took some time and we were becoming impatient. There were about ten paying customers aged three to seven and the older boys aged ten to twelve were the exhibitors. When, finally, the film started, it was upside down and we could not follow it. We were offered no redress, simply told to turn our heads sideways, otherwise shut up and go home. Needless to say, the cashier had already departed with the proceeds.

As we got a little older, we listened to a Mullard three-band radio set and when I was about ten we could receive music on long wave from the American Forces Network, AFN. We laughed at the Jack Benny show and enjoyed Glenn Miller, Les Brown and his band of Renown. A favourite was Tommy Dorsey who was introducing a new singer – Frank Sinatra. We listened to Dinah Shore, Judy Garland, Tony Martin, and Bing Crosby. One of our favourite shows was 'Luncheon from Munchin', which beat the heck out of Radio Éireann.

◆

The thirties was a decade when the Irish Free State got moving. British Prime Minister Lloyd George had commented on our independence, 'Give them a little time and they'll come crawling back.' No country had departed from the British Empire since America in 1783, and it was doubted by the British that the Irish would succeed. Sometime later, when India decided to leave the Empire, I believe their leaders came to Ireland to discuss protocol and seek advice on procedures.

Our nation's leaders were far-sighted, heroic planners who, having witnessed the birth of a nation, were prepared and able to lay the foundation for its healthy development. A national programme of building new schools was inaugurated. The Irish Hospitals Sweepstake was established to run regular sweepstakes on major races. It was a huge success; gambling was illegal in England and the USA, and many were only too keen to risk their money. A strong team was sent to America to organise the Sweepstake. Agents to sell the tickets were established everywhere, secretly overseas and openly in Ireland. Duffy's of the Diamond became an agent, and supplied punters local and overseas for many years. Money flooded into Ireland and although some may have found itself into the promoter's pockets, enough was delivered to build twenty new hospitals throughout the country.

Meanwhile, a team of engineers was working with the German industrial giant Siemens to build what was probably the most modern hydroelectric generating power station in the world at that time. It would supply a high-voltage grid system bringing three-phase 380 Volt and single-phase 220 Volt AC to the entire country. Harnessing the waters of the mighty Shannon, this national electrification program was known simply as the 'Shannon scheme'. At that time, we were on 110V DC from a local supplier.

Although we were living a quiet, protected life, all of Europe was in turmoil and getting worse. My earliest memory was a piece of history, witnessed from my bedroom window! – the return of the Irish Brigade from the Spanish Civil War. This war started in 1936, ended in March 1939, and was a particularly vicious affair in which many foreign nationals volunteered for different ideological reasons. General Franco's army was helped by Hitler and was perceived to be fascist, while the nationalist side was betrayed as being partly Communist. Pictures of brutal bombings of cities by Franco's German allies aroused sympathy, and volunteers arrived to oppose Franco. At home, Eoin O'Duffy, the former Chief of Staff of the IRA and in 1922 the first Commissioner of the Garda, had been sacked by De Valera.

An admirer of Mussolini, O'Duffy had formed a National Guard which used the Mussolini Roman straight arm salute and wore blue shirt uniforms – the 'Blue Shirts'. When the movement was outlawed, it merged into the new Fine Gael party with O'Duffy its leader for a very short time before resigning.

17

He reappeared in 1936 and organised the Irish Brigade to fight on Franco's side. Promoting himself to the rank of General, he led seven hundred men to Spain where he was not well-regarded. Described by a Spanish general as an Operetta General, it was said he, 'cost Franco a fortune and injured more of his own men than the enemy.' After one poorly-executed engagement Franco sent him home. Undeterred, O'Duffy claimed that the venture was a success and marched his men into Monaghan town in a victory parade. The massed ranks of men carrying flaming torches and marching to the beat of drums frightened me and I subsequently had nightmares. O'Duffy left politics and quietly disappeared from view after that.

With the Spanish Civil War ending, something cataclysmic happened – the world went to war.

CHAPTER 2
THE EMERGENCY

I FIRST BECAME AWARE of the reality of World War II when my father, normally a peaceful man, was sent to war with the British in North Monaghan. That day, as I walked home from school for my lunch, I could see that something serious was happening. The air raid siren on the Courthouse was wailing, the streets were buzzing with shock and rumor. Men were running around looking worried, groups gathered at street corners wanting to know what was happening.

I ran the rest of the way home and found the shop closed. Inside, the maid, the shop girls, and my mother were saying the Rosary in tears. Dad was in his bedroom putting on his uniform. The British had invaded us, crossing unopposed from Armagh and were advancing towards Monaghan. We all watched anxiously as my dad mounted his bike and cycled bravely off to join the Monaghan Brigade. We said another Rosary, and I went back to school.

When I returned that afternoon, my dad was home again, puffed up with pride at having defended the country and showing no inclination to take off his uniform. Never one to miss out on a good story he proudly elaborated on how the Monaghan soldiers had swiftly prepared to engage an enemy but were unable to find one. What had happened, was a British platoon on border control in Armagh had taken a wrong turn and inadvertently crossed into the Free State. The local Garda Sergeant quite properly dialled an emergency to Monaghan barracks who sounded the alarm and called for mobilization. Meanwhile, the Sergeant had pointed out his mistake to an embarrassed officer and the British retreated. They had left long before the local Defence Force arrived.

Earlier that year, in August 1939, my mother went to visit her sister in Manchester, England. She brought my eldest sister Carmel with her. They had hardly started their holiday when an announcement on the wireless warned all aliens and non-British personnel to leave the countryThey caught the boat train out of Manchester's Victoria Station on 1 September and crossed from Liverpool to Dublin, arriving home on 2 September. On 1 September, our Taoiseach De Valera had secured the agreement of the Reich Government to respect Ireland's neutrality. On the following day, 3 September, Mr Neville Chamberlain declared war on Germany. Phew!

As of 3 September, England had a war, Germany had a war, most of the world had a war, but Ireland had 'The Emergency'. As a neutral country, we were fighting with no one but had to suffer the effects of war on our economy and lifestyle. Portugal, another neutral country, also had no war; they had 'The Blackout'. That said, the Emergency kept us on our toes for six long years and beyond.

For the first period, nothing much happened and prudent householders built up their stores of provisions. We bought in two chests of tea, two sacks of sugar and some sacks of flour. Dad bought in two lorry loads of coal, which we supplemented each summer with turf and wood.

Everyone was issued with ration cards and we children sometimes bargained our sugar ration for money or sweets with Mum and Dad who had a sweet tooth. All sugar was weighed on our shop scales into individual portions and the bags were named. When setting the table, it was funny to see six or more brown paper bags on the table, each named for someone with a month's supply of sugar. I can remember no case of dispute or 'borrowing'. It must have been the wartime spirit.

The grain husks in flour were too valuable to discard; it became illegal to sieve them out, so white bread became unobtainable. We were obliged to eat wholemeal brown bread and we did not like it. Compared to Mr Sherry's white batch loaf, the wholemeal bread was coarse and, to us children, sour-tasting. Our small supply of white flour was soon eaten and we survived on coarse brown bread for nearly five years. Once or twice towards the end of the war, Mum used a flour sieve to remove the husks. She mixed in an egg and some currants – a real treat.

Little by little as the Emergency progressed, rations became tighter and we fell back more on our own resources. We had long been self-sufficient in food and were an important supplier to Britain, but we needed to import wheat, fruit, tea, oil, and petrol.

Prior to World War II, the Irish fleet had shrunk from over a hundred vessels to fifty-six, so we had become largely dependent on foreign shipping. When war broke out foreign shippers would no longer sail in dangerous waters, and Britain could no longer run the risk to their ships supplying Ireland. About sixteen extra ships were bought by the Free State at that time with some considerable difficulty. Inevitably, the war began to impact on our neutrality, our standards of living, and our safety.

In the early days of hostilities our ships sailed within convoys but after several disastrous passages it was decided to sail alone as neutrals, although that decision was reviewed from time to time, in the light of higher insurance charges by Lloyd's for unprotected ships.

It was a principal of convoy practice not to delay if one of their ships was sinking but Irish ships did so and rescued 534 seamen. The Irish ships were unarmed and decorated with the tricolour and EIRE written largely on both sides and on decks. This was fairly well respected, although sixteen ships were sunk by attacks mainly by German U-boats or bombers from both sides.

There were some interesting encounters between U-boats and our ships, two of which are recounted here, with acknowledgements to Wikipedia:

The *Irish Willow* was stopped by *U-753* with instructions to send over the Master and papers for proof of neutrality. As the Captain was from Belfast, the Chief Officer went with the excuse that Capt. Shank was too infirm. It was 16 March 1942 and Chief Officer Harry Cullen referred to St Patrick's Day in the morning. They were treated to schnapps in the conning tower and given a bottle of Cognac to bring back to the ailing captain.

On 20 March 1943, the *U-638* stopped the *Irish Elm*, seeking papers of neutrality. When Chief Officer Patrick Hennessy gave his address as Dun Laoghaire, German Commander Henrik Bernbek enquired, 'Is the strike still on in Downey's?' Downey's was a pub near the harbour, where a strike ran from 1939 for fourteen years.

The Irish Mercantile Fleet carried over a million tons of wheat, coal, phosphates, tobacco, and newsprint to keep Ireland supplied and bolstered the government's determination to continue our neutrality, which otherwise would have failed.

In fact, our neutrality was secretly but firmly weighted in favour of the Allies.

It is difficult now to fully understand the precarious position of Ireland in 1939. We were only seventeen years free after seven hundred years of domination by a huge empire, still poor and struggling to establish a viable economy. Our relationship with Britain was confused, having fought a trade war which had only just been settled in 1938. The British wanted access to our food which was welcome but the bitterness of the Anglo-Irish and Civil Wars was very real. If we had agreed to join with Britain it probably would have led to a resurgence of the civil war.

In the event it was handled masterfully. We had negotiated a peace treaty with Germany in September 1939, an action supported by the Dáil, with the exception of James Dillon, who resigned from Fine Gael on the issue. The truth is that we were neutral, but more on the British side.

While we refused to close the German embassy, we did insist that they surrender their radio transmitter which meant their using telegraphs for communication, which would have been easy listening for the British. All our coastal stations reported to Dublin by radio, allowing the British to listen to our reports for local forecasts – as could the Germans, but they were so far away as to be irrelevant. This support by the coastal stations was especially highlighted in June 1945 by a special occurrence.

On the night of 3 June 1944, Maureen Flavin was on duty in the Post Office in Black Sod Bay, Co Mayo. It was her 21st birthday and she was taking barometer readings instead of partying in New York as she had planned. When she joined the Post Office, she was surprised to learn that her duties included weather readings on a prescribed schedule, but she found it easy and quickly mastered it. A conscientious lady, she took care with the accuracy of her barometer readings. This was as well because they would be strongly challenged. As part of a co-operation agreement, the Free State kept the British informed about weather forecasts but not the Germans.

Unknown to Maureen, on the south coast of England, Warlord, the largest invasion force in history – 160,000 men, 5000 ships and 11,000 planes – was poised ready for the go signal from General Eisenhower. He was in a quandary. His original planned date for the invasion of Normandy had been 5 June, when Maureen's readings arrived indicating a storm on that day. Caught between meteorologists and generals, it was a tough call, but he postponed the invasion with the prospect of a delay for weeks. The surprise element would be gone, giving the Germans time to prepare defences. There was just one window between 6 and 7 June when the moon and tides were suitable. If only?

On 4 June, Maureen noted the barometer rising and forecast a window of weather on 6 June. The Germans knew there was a large storm coming. Unaware of the small local high, they thought an invasion wouldn't happen and several senior officers including Rommel took a few days off.

The invasion of Normandy took place on 6 June thanks to Maureen Flavin.

Irish security authorities were on the highest alert for downed pilots, infiltrators or spies together with possible dissidents, which included IRA personnel. Several plots against national security and neutrality were harshly dealt with and all personnel imprisoned in the Curragh. Allied air force and marine personnel were discreetly released to Northern Ireland. Downed German pilots were comfortably detained in army quarters.

Author's note: During my service in the British Merchant Navy, I met several seamen who had been looked after by the Irish, including a First Mate Scully, who had been rescued from a sinking ship and landed in Galway before travelling to Northern Ireland.

George Thomas, my radio tutor in wireless college, Manchester, had been a Flight Sgt on bombing raids over Germany. He told me how a strong radio signal from the RTE broadcasting station 'Athlone' had been a useful beacon for night navigation, which the German bombers used. When requested by the

British, 'Athlone' relocated to South Wales which misled the Germans diverting them to Snowdonia where British fighters were waiting. Later, 'Athlone' again relocated to North Wales, diverting the Germans to the Yorkshire Moors. Thomas informed me that at one stage there were three 'Athlone' broadcasting, confusing the Germans and possibly resulting in the Dublin bombing.

Conversely, when the Germans asked Switzerland to reduce the signal strength of Helvetia, their equally powerful radio signal, or change location, the request was refused.

The secret 'Donegal Corridor' was a narrow strip of airspace over South Donegal/Leitrim that allowed RAF flying boats from an airbase on Loch Erne to use a shorter route to the North Atlantic. This violation of Irish neutrality had resulted from a meeting between Mr de Valera and the English government representative in Dublin who agreed the concession. The extra flying hours gave the patrols extra time to reach far out into the Atlantic seeking U-boats and protecting convoys. The concession proved extremely useful, with nine U-boats sunk and a sighting of the Bismarck, marking its position which led to its sinking.

Many years later when I lived in Dorking, an English friend, John Parnell, told me how he was stationed on Lough Erne just across the border from Ballyshannon, part of the North Atlantic submarine patrol. He and his friends would don a civilian raincoat over their RAF gear and steal into Ballyshannon for a few pints or to buy what luxury items presented themselves. Strictly speaking, they should have been interned had they been identified, but Irish neutrality was liberal towards the British. John, the pilot, started his patrol flying out over Donegal Bay. The crew of John's Short Sunderland aircraft included a Jamaican rear gunner whose duties included transmission of signals by Aldus Lamp. Each night John noticed an exchange of Aldus signals between the Jamaican and the lighthouse on Innis Murray in County Sligo. Too preoccupied at first, John eventually got around to enquiring from his rear gunner what messages were being trafficked. 'I didn't start it, that bugger called me a bollocks and I replied stupid bollocks.' Over the months the rude name calling had expanded as both signallers sought to outdo the other in rudeness. It helped to pass the time.

Coincidently, another friend, Peter Moffat, also flew Short Sunderlands out of Lough Erne on the North Atlantic U-boat patrol. In three years they were only once called into action. They saw a target surfacing in a flurry of white foam, immediately dived to the attack and scored a direct hit – result, one dead whale. My children will remember Peter, who brought his scuba gear into our pool to teach our children scuba diving.

Roosevelt and Churchill growled and grumbled, both considering invasions of Ireland but fortunately at different times. De Valera had arrested senior IRA members, including several who favoured German invasions into Northern Ireland. Irish diplomats and bureaucrats worked well with the Allies in diplomatic circles; this was especially true in Europe, where the Irish diplomatic personnel cooperated with Bill Donovan's OSS, to the point where he described them as quasi-US spies.

One of the problems that beset Ireland's one-sided neutrality was that its subtleties were beyond the understanding of the US Minister in Dublin, David Gray. He simply didn't understand the need for Irish discretion and personally distrusted De Valera. Fortunately, most concerned officials could easily see his opinions as ill-judged, and he did little harm.

Left to ourselves, we improvised, not always successfully; such as when my mother decided to supply her family with a banana substitute. One of the ladies' magazines – *Good Housekeeping* or *Woman and Home* – gave her a recipe, which required Mum to boil parsnips, mash vigorously and mix in a small bottle of banana essence. Where she got the essence, I can't imagine. At any rate, it tasted foul. We mostly hated parsnips anyway, but to have to mix them with a foul-tasting additive and spread it on bread was beyond revolting – it was sick-making. Normally a martinet about eating what you were given, Mum eased up on this one and enjoyed the joke herself. I only met one other victim of this recipe: Kay O'Neill, wife of the Bank of Ireland manager in Sligo, also remembered the incident, both of us war victims. At our age we hardly missed oranges and other tropical fruits, which was as well because it would be six long years before we would see them again.

While we missed many imported products, the Free State was fortunate to be self-sufficient in food with just adequate supplies of butter, ham, bacon and beef, all of which were severely rationed in Northern Ireland. However, with few mills we were seriously short of clothing materials, all readily available in the North with its huge mills. It was not surprising that a smuggling trade quickly developed between the two states, to address these mutual needs.

My mother returned to her old IRA ways and became an adept smuggler of cloth. Once or twice a year, lightly clad, she would catch the train to Armagh. On her return she had developed into a fat woman with many yards of material wrapped around her waist, material for Tom Kelly the tailor, or the dressmaker.

In the reverse direction, our shop staff received many requests for chocolate and food provisions – but how to get it over the border? This was solved when one of our customers, a police sergeant, found it necessary to meet with his Northern Ireland colleagues every Thursday. A police car was never going to be searched by the Customs. The good sergeant became our courier, for which we supplied him with cigarettes for the rest of the war.

Although tropical fruit was no longer available in our shop, we were able to sell home-grown apples, pears and plums and we did a good trade in those. Inevitably some fruit became over-ripe and had to be dumped, which always offended my father. He also noted that we were giving our family waste food to a collector who used it to feed pigs. He resolved to do something to correct this and soon erected a small shed at the bottom of the yard. I arrived home from school one afternoon to find a lovely little piglet in our yard. I was, of course, delighted. Dad knew little about feeding pigs, let alone cleaning up their dirt. I think he may have overfed it because the little piglet quickly grew into a large, fat pig. The floor of the pig shed, like the rest of our yard, consisted of cobblestones and Dad was concerned about hygiene and the difficulty of keeping it clean. A frustrated builder, he was always ready for an opportunity to show off his skills, so he cemented the floor of the pig shed, finishing his work with a wonderfully smooth surface. Bad move! Within a week, the big fat pig slipped on the smooth cement and broke a leg. We sent for our veterinarian friend, Larry McIllhargey, and laughed so much that Dad never bought another pig. From then on, the shed was used for storing turf.

At the back of our shop was a small den, half-hidden behind a tall desk. It had several chairs and a radio, and was heated by a pot-bellied cast iron stove, aptly named Inferno, which consumed unlimited quantities of anything combustible: saw-dust, timber, coal or turf. It provided the only heating to the shop. In cold weather it burned both night and day, and with the damper open it could be stoked with fuel until the entire carcass glowed a dull ominous red.

During the day, this 'back of the shop' was used by Mum to meet 'Commercial Travellers' and pay their accounts. After tea Mum joined the family and the maids in the back kitchen to supervise homework and housework. My father would then occupy the den for a nightly review of the world's affairs with his cronies.

One evening my father asked me to join him at the back of the shop to hear something important. Dad's cronies, Joe Turley, Editor of the Northern Standard, and Owen Connelly, the County Registrar, had already gathered. They were all clustered anxiously around our small battery-powered radio.

A critical stage had been reached in the Allied strategies. As the Atlantic corridor became more vulnerable to mounting German U-boat attacks, the Allies were becoming increasingly desperate to get the use of our ports. Critically positioned to help control the North Atlantic and the Northern approaches to the Baltic, Churchill had once again formally requested access to them for use in major naval defence initiatives being planned to seize back control of the North Atlantic. This would effectively bring Ireland into the conflict in a serious way. As the demand had become public knowledge De Valera indicated that he would reply to the demand in a public broadcast to both the Irish people and to the world.

The Shannon Scheme had not yet reached Monaghan – the local direct current (DC) power supply from a local diesel generator was low voltage, 110 volts on a good day. The radio was powered by a wet lead-acid battery, which had to be regularly recharged at McCoy's bicycle shop in Dublin Street. We always had two batteries so that one could be in use while the other was being charged. One of my regular chores was to bring the batteries down to Mc Coy's for recharging.

The gang of three used to sit each night picking up news from Radio Éireann and BBC Belfast. This night there was particular tension in the group and I tucked in beside my dad as we waited to hear what might decide the future of the country. We learned afterwards that Churchill had promised a deal on returning Northern Ireland to the Free State after the war. We knew that De Valera was about to announce his decision. Of course, he said, 'No way,' using the British occupation of the six northern counties as a reason. I was probably eight at the time, and felt very grown up to sit with the town elders.

By now we young ones were becoming aware of the excitement of the war. Young Monaghan men were signing up. Some became fighter pilots and a McCaldin gained a commission in the infantry. Many young children were evacuated from Belfast to Monaghan and our school classes became larger with refugees. From our parents we gathered that things were going badly for the Allies.

There were many visible signs of the war apart from the shortage of food. The few cars on the roads had their headlights fitted with blackout masks, which only allowed a slit of light to emerge. We were all required to buy and hang black-out blinds. I remember some lorries were fuelled by gas. Anti-tank barriers were erected on the road to the North. These consisted of huge cement blocks with steel girders angled forward toward the enemy.

My father patriotically joined the LDF (Local Defence Force), later FCA (Forsa Cosanta Aitiul), a similar version of Dad's Army. He wore a Boys Brigade type beret, a Sam Browne belt and large brown boots. They drilled in the Market Yard and occasionally paraded through the town.

My dad's LDF uniform was dowdy, rough serge and I was envious of Mr Mullen's uniform. He was a private in the ARP (Air Raid Patrol) and as the nearest sergeant was in Dundalk, he was the senior local officer. When our forces paraded through the town on St. Patrick's Day or on days of a Feis (festival) he always led his troop with panache.

This all went wrong for him one day when the ARP gave a demonstration of their prowess. The occasion was a Feis or a sports day held in the grounds of the new CBS school. Mr

Mullen explained that the ARP would demonstrate the power of an incendiary bomb and would show how to control and extinguish it. Some cement blocks were carefully placed in the centre of the new concrete playground to form a safe platform for the incendiary. Mr Mullen positioned his men in a circle to hold back the spectators. There was a great air of expectancy, even apprehension in the crowd as Mr Mullen ignited the device. It glowed with the white heat of burning phosphorous and we were suitably impressed. When the flame was well established, Mr Mullen and his troop applied their fire hoses to extinguish the firebomb. The incendiary burned more fiercely than ever. More fire extinguishers were applied yet the incendiary blossomed. By now the ARP were looking confused and beginning to panic. They brought on more fire extinguishers, all to no avail. The cement blocks were beginning to disintegrate and the crowd were beginning to enjoy a fiasco. To the accompaniment of cat calls and derisive laughter the incendiary fell through the cracked cement block and started to crack the new concrete playground. I think the bomb was still glowing when we all went home. The cracks in the playground remained there for years.

We saw very little of the war, an occasional barrage balloon in free flight causing some excitement but little else until the day our school was buzzed by the RAF.

In the early forties aircraft were a rarity; indeed, I'm not sure if I had even seen one until the day when a Spitfire circled over the town. What excitement! Class work was forgotten as we all rushed to the windows as the Spitfire circled, coming lower and lower. It was clearly not aggressive, just showing off. Finally, it came so low that it was level with our school windows (the school was on a hill). It made three passes over the schoolyard and then roared off towards Northern Ireland. Not only was this jaw-droppingly exciting, it was highly dangerous, a breach of our neutrality, and caused a diplomatic incident. Many years later, we heard that the pilot was a local man and that he was discharged for his actions.

It would be incorrect to say that I was pro-German during the war. In fact, at ten years old, I didn't have any strong views. The fact was that the German S.S. uniforms – black leather with that brim down black hat and all with white piping – was much more attractive than the green serge blouses of the Brits. There was glamour about their Iron Cross Gestapo insignia and most of their matching songs. Francie Duffy, from Dublin St., I and a group of other young boys formed a closet Nazi corp. A supply of ex-army insignia was filtering back from the war zones and we collected a few German badges. We learned a little of the German language and played at practicing the goose step and the Hitler salute.

The only pro-active step we ever took was the day after Italy capitulated. A group of us followed poor old Mr and Mrs Malocca down the town booing and calling them 'yellow eye ties.'

At the height of the war my mother took us on holiday for a month. She had booked Woodbine Cottage in Bundoran's West End. There would be eight in the party this time: Mum with Nellie Coogan – one of our maids – plus six children and two dogs. We travelled through Northern Ireland on the Great Northern Railway train. I can still remember the hostility that emanated from the N.I. security men who boarded the train at the border crossing. They came in pairs into our compartment, tall in their black B Special uniform, large revolvers on their hips. Their attitude was insolent and provocative. A mother with a maid and six children going to Bundoran hardly posed a security threat, yet their attitude clearly upset my mother and frightened us. An odd recollection.

I had saved up four shillings and six pence for the month's holiday and it lasted well. An H.P. ice cream slider cost one penny. It was served between two small pieces of white shiny cardboard, as wafers were not available. I could get five 'Conversation Lozenges' for a farthing (a quarter of a penny).

The war was more evident in Bundoran. There was the wreck of a British plane, which had crashed on the sand dunes to the north of Rogey. One day, a German seaplane landed in the bay – out of fuel. Under our laws of neutrality, the crew were given two hours to buy fuel and depart, which they did. Meanwhile the Irish Army would have informed the British in Northern Ireland, who were waiting for it to leave Irish territorial waters before shooting it down.

Our shop sold newspapers and my Dad was always ready to alert me to a major headline. I clearly remember the Irish Press headline 'D-Day.' The other memorable ones included V. Day, Atomic Bomb Dropped, and V. E. Day.

Our shop carried a full range of magazines. Many of these were British or American and well-informed on the war. They included *London Illustrated News*, *Illustrated*, *Look*, *Life*, *Saturday Evening Post*, and *Picture Post*. As the war drew to a close, I became aware of the horrors that neutrality had sheltered us from. I saw my first picture of a fully naked woman in an article on Auschwitz where she was being deloused.

Bananas started arriving back. Ships coming north from South Africa or the West Indies stopped at the Canary Islands and loaded the decks with bananas for a society who didn't know what they were. A homecoming sailor handed a banana to a little girl who burst out crying, while her mother thumped the sailor. Another man in our shop said he saw a child eating a banana with the skin on.

I was walking home from school when I saw the excitement outside McCaldins over a window full of oranges. I rushed home and my mother gave me money to buy a dozen. I can't remember how many I ate but I had diarrhoea that night.

The war was over.

CHAPTER 3

OUT OF THE NEST AND DINNER WITH THE PRESIDENT OF IRELAND

MOVING INTO PRIMARY SCHOOL was the first foot out of the nest. Most boys spent five years in primary school, but I only spent four. Because of two years of illness, I went straight into second class to catch up.

Primary schools in Ireland were mainly run and taught by the Christian Bros, a religious order who dedicated their lives to teaching Catholic boys.

The background to education in Ireland had been the conditions imposed by the Penal Laws, established by the British in 1695 and strengthened in 1709. Catholic schoolteachers were prohibited, and it was illegal to send Catholic children to school other than to a Protestant school. It was planned that children going to Church of England schools would become loyal, learn English, and change religion.

These despicable laws finally ended in 1829. The Christian Bros were started in 1802 by Edmund Ignatius Rice, later beatified, to serve a community still reeling from the dreadful effects of penal times. The Brothers had taken a vow of celibacy and obedience. They were, of course, normal men, and some were more suited to the job than others. I met both types in my time there.

I was not long in the second class, aged about eight, when we were brought out to the nearby sports field. The teacher informed us that each Wednesday would be given over to football, with fitness training each Friday morning. This was good news, better than classwork. It was time for my father to buy me football boots and runners. All of a sudden, school wasn't so bad.

Brother King took us in third and fourth classes. He was a fat, mellow Cork man, very affable and a good teacher. He taught us to 'burn everything British except their coal.' He gathered a number of pupils who collected lead soldiers as a hobby, and as I had a collection of several regiments, I joined the club. Many Saturdays we would gather in a classroom, clear back the desks and draw battle lines with chalk on the floor. We fought Crimean and Peninsular wars under Brother King's direction – great fun.

In fifth class we had a narcissistic brother with carefully Brylcreemed hair and the smell of talcum powder and aftershave. He shouldn't have been allowed to teach, as he was a menace both physically and emotionally. With an uncontrollable temper, he threw objects at pupils: wooden-backed dusters and once a complete box of chalk. Several times he opened the windows and physically ejected students. In fairness, he was aware that we were on the ground floor, but it was still a good drop, maybe five feet. It was a relief to move to secondary school.

The Brothers all used leather straps to punish us when we needed it. This practice was probably inherited from earlier days and was no worse than canes used in other schools. Some teachers used wide straps which were not so painful, some used the more punitive narrow half-inch straps and aimed for the fingertips which stung more than on the flat palm.

In spite of these experiences, my time at the CBS was a happy one, where I learned much and gently started to mature my social skills.

In recent years there have been shocking revelations about questionable relationships between Brothers and pupils. I was never aware of any such misconduct.

At about this time the school had the benefit of the new headmaster – a Brother Coughlan, who had been transferred back to Ireland from Buenos Aires and brought with him a positive desire to raise the cultural level of the school. He organised receptions for the school Governors and for the Bishop. We were taught choral singing – in Irish, of course. We were uniquely taught to sing 'The Blue Danube' in Irish, a rare party piece. At one recital for the school Governors we sang a medley by Stephen Foster which included the song 'Poor Old Joe'. My father hugely enjoyed the irony as the three governors were Joe Duffy, Joe Turley and Joe Corr.

My mother visited Dublin occasionally and sometimes she brought me, aged ten or twelve, with her. It was exciting to see the bustle of the big city, the noisy trams and so many buses.

At the junction of Westmorland Street and D'Olier Street with O'Connell Bridge stood a tall policeman on a pulpit wearing a Kaiser Wilhelm-type helmet and white gloves. Long before traffic lights, he imperiously directed the flow of traffic, cars, bicycles, horse-drawn carts, buses and trams. These policemen were relics of the Dublin Metropolitan Police even though the original British force had been absorbed into the Irish Civic Guards in the 1920s. They were very impressive.

The best treat of all was 'The Pillar', as Nelson's Pillar was known. We paid 6d to climb its 168 spiral steps to a height of nearly forty metres. I did so twice. The Pillar was built forty years before Trafalgar Square's Nelson column, and in its day was the tallest Doric column in the world. It was blown up by the IRA in 1966, probably as a fifty-year memorial of 1916.

My two older sisters, Carmel and Maura, had attended the St Louis Convent. My mother was involved in a number of religious organisations while my father, a Town and County Councillor, was often on the top table when the nuns held a reception to announce or celebrate some occasion.

It was not a surprise therefore that Mum was asked to have one of her sons help as an usher at the annual Gilbert and Sullivan operetta. Aged about thirteen, I got the gig. My family hired a dinner jacket, dressed me up in a black tie and sent me off to *The Mikado*. I can clearly define this as the time when I first started to become aware of how nice girls were. I was lucky enough to get the nod again the following year but after that I may have become too mature to be released among the St Louis girls and I wasn't asked a third time.

At school in fourth year, our Shakespeare play was *As You Like It*; our Latin study book was Caesar's *Gallic Wars*, Book 1. I sat my Intermediate Exam, passed it and went home for a long hot summer. I didn't know that I wouldn't be coming back to the Christian Bros school. It was 1948.

The next four years were to change my life fundamentally, I believe for the better. The whole wide world was beckoning, and I was impatient to get there. My dad had died in 1947 and I was growing up developing my personal strengths and helping with running the house and the shop. I particularly liked working part-time in the shop.

Swimming became my main interest. Earlier my father had joined with a number of other businessmen to start up a private swimming club at Lamb's Lake and to build a very fine diving deck and dressing rooms. The deck area was about five metres by five metres, with springboards at one and two metres and a diving deck at three metres, as well as an aluminium slide about four metres long. The lake was fed by springs and was spotlessly clean with underwater clarity of about five metres. A raft was anchored about twenty-five metres from the deck. As a private club, it attracted a nice crowd and was a great social centre for swimmers. I had a great friend, Eddie Casey, who was on the Clongowes swimming team. He taught me the butterfly stroke and swam with me throughout the summer. Another swimming companion was Roy Baldwin, an ESB superintendent.

These and other companions were important company as we often were the only people swimming across a very deep lake. The old folk claimed that it was bottomless, but many years later when I had become an accomplished snorkeler, I touched bottom at about forty feet.

I cannot remember how I met my first crush, a beautiful young girl, the daughter of a respected house painter. She was a Protestant but the family were welcoming to me and raised no objections to our keeping company. It was all innocent, movies and walks and holding hands –very little kissing. I made one bad mistake. My mother had been in Dublin for a few days and arrived back earlier than expected. She met us strolling hand in hand in Church Square as she was going to evening prayer. Her face darkened with displeasure; she made no effort to be introduced to the young lady, and glowered, 'I'll see you when you get home.'

Two weeks later I was informed that I was going to St Macartan's College in September. I believe the matrons of Monaghan had been talking to each other. Not only was I going to board, so were Lorcan Ronaghan, Paul McCormack, and Francie Duffy, old school friends for many years. Another neighbour from the Diamond came to the school the following year, Liam Murray. I am blessed that Lorcan and Liam are alive, in good health and enjoying life, a true bonus after nearly eighty years.

St Macartan's was a truly spartan place. Although fitted with central heating pipes and radiators, these were never heated during my time at the school. The water in hand basins was never heated and we only had two showers during my two years there. This was when we had home football games with St Patrick's College, Cavan, and St Patrick's College, Armagh.

The Dean was ready for what he referred to as 'the Monaghan gang', and he split us into different dormitories. He placed me right beside the main dormitory door – very visible.

It was a miserable place. I could see the lights of Monaghan, only a mile away. I missed home cooking and I was frozen most of the time. We put sheets of newspaper between the blankets to help us keep warm in bed on winter nights when ice formed on the inside of dormitory windows. Washing in icy cold water wasn't pleasant. Combing my hair, I learned to use Bragan Hair Oil, named after our water supply from the Bragan mountains.

Bad experiences included being ducked into a barrel of cold water by way of welcome to the school – a centuries old tradition – as well as dealing with some sixth-year bullies. But there were better memories, such as playing Gaelic football for the college in the Ulster Championships, and acting in the annual play, where I was cast as the fast-living man-about-town in *The Private Secretary*, a comedy. We also formed the Monaghan Glee Club and put on a revue.

One of the positives was the size and nature of my class. There were only twenty pupils in the class, including the four Monaghan boys. The majority of the others were boffins, bright, intelligent, gentle, and good company.

The sixth grade was rather different, about thirty-two pupils with a number of bullies and philistines. Our class felt it necessary to negotiate with them to clarify that as a senior grade we insisted on being treated with respect. My playing on the senior football team was a great help to me personally and won me considerable respect.

St Macartan's was founded in the middle of the nineteenth century and many of its archaic traditions dated from then. Not only were radios not allowed; incredibly, all newspapers and magazines were also banned.

Another tradition was to elect the senior and junior prefects in the first week of the new term. Details of these 'free elections' were not announced, and I am sure that they were totally fixed by the college President and Dean. The Senior Prefect sat on a raised dais in front of the large study hall facing his schoolmates. The Junior Prefect sat on a similar dais at the rear of the hall. Generally, they had nothing to do except to growl if whispering became a nuisance. A stern glance from the Senior Prefect was usually enough to control things. Additionally, the Dean would snoop in on silent shoes and glide noiselessly around the hall.

I was pleased to be picked for the Senior Football Team and enjoyed playing against Armagh and Cavan. As well as the excitement and the adrenaline rush, it meant days out, good feeds and hot showers. Because I had been seen to play moderately well, I was also picked for a place on the County Monaghan Minor team – quite an honour.

My classmate and long-term friend Lorcan reminded me of an escapade that nearly got us expelled. On one occasion, when there was a serious Gaelic football competition, we reckoned that the priests would all be watching as it was their area of interest. We decided to slip out to the town and watch a movie. We were missed, causing great panic with telephone calls to our homes, so when we returned, we were seriously in the doghouse. It is Lorcan's opinion that we could have been expelled that night, except that I was due to play against St Patrick's, Cavan, on the following day.

My two years were drawing to a close. I had a bad relationship with the Dean, and when I was caught smoking cigarettes for the third time, I was sent home during the revision, only allowed back to sit my leaving certificate. I was pleased to get two Honours, Latin and English, with passes in four other subjects.

In St Macartan's, students were expected to consider the priesthood and I never heard of any career guidance available. Indeed, there was very little reference to the subject anywhere so I asked my mother what career I should do. She only knew of three options: the priesthood, medicine, or dentistry. I couldn't imagine myself as a priest, so I opted for dentistry. I applied to UCD for admission and was successful.

Some of my classmates excelled in the final exam with outstanding results. Sean Clarkin came first in Ireland; Peadar Livingstone came second with Cahal O'Neill fourth. Irral Ward came in the top ten. An incredible achievement for a small rural college.

Many years later, I met Sean Clarkin who was by then a priest and working for the Archbishop in Armagh, responsible for administering applications for marriage nullity. I can now reveal his sad admission that the procedure was deliberately planned to procrastinate to a point where things might improve, not requiring a decision. The last thing they wanted was a rapid decree.

I also met Peadar Livingstone, then a parish priest in County Fermanagh. He had written a history of County Monaghan, the first serious history since the *Annals of the Four Masters*. Helen obtained a copy, had it signed and dedicated to me for my birthday present. The poor man subsequently took his own life. Cahal O'Neill became Company Secretary of the Gypsum Company. Sadly, Irral Ward died suddenly in his twenties.

I have rarely felt drawn to go back to St Macartan's since leaving. In 1950, a group of us attended a past pupils dinner and met some of the students. We were obliquely informed that the Past Pupils Union would not be encouraged to make professional vocational presentations to the boys, as it might distract them from possible religious vocations.

Many years later, Lorcan and I made two career presentations to the senior form, Lorcan on Pharmacy and I on Entrepreneurship. When we had supper with two young priests afterwards, I was shocked to learn that they were arch-Republicans, total supporters of the IRA.

I had turned sixteen in September 1949 and received a present from the family of a suit and tails, complete with white tie and white waistcoat. I joined my sister Carmel and a whole bunch of friends from Monaghan at the Hunt Ball in Armagh and later at a dress dance in Monaghan. Carmel had taught me the three-step, and having a good sense of rhythm I rapidly became a reasonable dancer. Social life quickened up as I got to know a number of girls my own age. We had great fun and went dancing in Armagh and Swan Park, Monaghan.

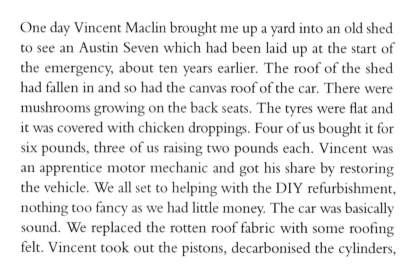

One day Vincent Maclin brought me up a yard into an old shed to see an Austin Seven which had been laid up at the start of the emergency, about ten years earlier. The roof of the shed had fallen in and so had the canvas roof of the car. There were mushrooms growing on the back seats. The tyres were flat and it was covered with chicken droppings. Four of us bought it for six pounds, three of us raising two pounds each. Vincent was an apprentice motor mechanic and got his share by restoring the vehicle. We all set to helping with the DIY refurbishment, nothing too fancy as we had little money. The car was basically sound. We replaced the rotten roof fabric with some roofing felt. Vincent took out the pistons, decarbonised the cylinders, cleaned out the pump and replaced the lube oil. We were all excited one day as we had a whip around to get cash and put in some petrol. After a few anxious moments and a series of snorts, it fired up.

There were lots of smiling faces on our neighbours as we drove it triumphantly around the town. There weren't many places to visit and we couldn't afford a lot of petrol so we didn't make much use of it. One wet Sunday we set out to Dundalk and on the way back we burst a tyre. We didn't have a spare, so we had to abandon it on the roadside. As I was packing my bags to go to UCD next day, I left Monaghan with little hope of its recovery. Without money to buy a replacement tyre, what could be done?

About a month later, I got a message that the car had been sold for £18 and would I like to use my share of the money to buy a quarter share in Radox, a racehorse? We ran it at the Phoenix Park races one night. The jockey was Celestine Maclin, brother of the motor mechanic Vincent. He thought it might win. I put my two weeks' allowance on it and it came in last. I lost track of events after that, but every so often I would receive £10 or so from its winnings. I learned later that it was running at point-to-point races against farm animals. Finally, it was sold as a point-to-point racer and I got quite a nice sum. That concluded my racehorse-owning phase which proved a bit of fun and quite rewarding financially.

Preparing for university, I arranged accommodation with a friend, Donal Ward, sharing one room. We were fortunate to find a nice landlady, Mrs Murphy, in no. 21, Vavasour Square, Sandymount. Donal got the single bed and I got the double – which got complicated later. My mother had visited Dublin several times, helping me with my domestic arrangements. She travelled by train and on one occasion as I was bidding her goodbye on the train in Amiens Street Station, Donal was seeing his mother off, at which point both ladies were leaning out of adjoining windows. I noted that Mrs Ward leaned down and kissed Donal, while my mother shook hands with me. That cameo made an indelible impression, as I realised that neither my father or mother had ever kissed or even hugged me. It was, of course, the remnants of Victorian behaviour, but I vowed then that I would kiss and hug my wife and children if I was lucky enough to win a family.

I had brought my bike to Dublin and cycled to college each day. I was studying the pre-dental course of chemistry, botany, zoology and physics. My allowance from mum was £14 per month and I soon settled into a good social life – in fact, too good by far.

There were dances in the Four Provinces and The Crystal Ballroom, which was my favourite. The resident band was the Johnny Devlin Band, with Fran Young on trombone and singer Rose Brennan, who would soon be headhunted to join the Joe Loss band in London. I also discovered McDaid's pub at this time, learned to like Guinness, met Brendan Behan and several other characters.

With hindsight, it is clear that I was out of my depth. I had just turned sixteen, an immature country lad coming from a seminary and now free to sow my wild oats. I was also studying a course which held no interest for me. Anyway, I dropped behind the studies, and finally gave up. I didn't even sit the exams.

My friend Donal Ward was in his second year in the arts faculty and was well established. Through him, I met a lot of interesting people. I used to attend the Literary and Historical, L&H, debating society on Saturday nights. Richie Ryan was Auditor that year, and had to handle a noisy Ulick O'Connor, a real character. He was so disruptive that he was banned from attending future debates. I was there the night that he appeared as his sister, and in a fine falsetto voice spoke up for 'her brother'. Members of the college boxing team surrounded 'her', and when she disrobed, they protected him as he withdrew rapidly.

Paul Callan had been in St Macartan' the year before me and spoke often at the L&H. I made my maiden speech there but wasn't really up to it. Paul later became a prominent barrister; Donal Barrington and Seamus Sorahan were even more successful. Gerry Charlton's brother Hugh was there having secured the Irish agency for the then little-known Sony. I don't think he made a go of it.

Donal Ward was a charming man and we got along very well until he started taking in strays. His brother Peader was out of work and we took him in on a temporary basis. Soon afterwards, Richie Ryan came to sleep with us temporarily. The problem was that the strays shared the double bed with me. If I remember correctly, Richie Ryan's father had thrown him out of his home over politics. All this overcrowding put pressure on our relationship and we had a bust-up, but we met amicably many years later.

One bizarre incident is worth recalling. Because I had a formal dress suit, tails, white waistcoat and white tie, I secured an invitation to meet the President of Ireland at Áras an Uachtaráin. I was friendly with an art student, Una McCullough, whose aunt was married to Seán T. O'Kelly. Una had been asked to make up a party to attend the 21st birthday of Princess Claudia von Habsburg. As I learned, the von Habsburgs were given sanctuary by the Irish government to protect them from the Nazis. By 1950 the Nazis were long gone, so I don't know why she was still there. The function was small, but formal. As no one offered any transport with my invitation I had to rely on my own bicycle and arrived in my tails. I was formally received by an aide de camp in army dress uniform, and introduced to Seán T., who was tiny beside his wife, a big, well-built woman.

I had to dance with Princess Claudia, who was much taller than me and not at all beautiful; theHabsburgs were never famous for their looks. However, I did enjoy a good dinner.

I hadn't admitted to my family that I hadn't sat the exams, and there was some talk of my repeating the year. I had lost my self-confidence, felt very guilty, and knew that our poor shop simply couldn't afford to pay for an expensive education. I didn't know what to do until Uncle Fred in Manchester threw me a lifeline. The Radio College in John Dalton Street was running a nine-month course to qualify students as radio officers. The thought of being an officer and a gentleman after nine months, rather than study for four or five years, was appealing. When I thought of sailing all over the world, I was jumping.

The deal was that my uncle and aunt would host me, leaving Mum to pay the modest school fees. The only problem was that the current course was now two months into the program. Could I catch up? Would they accept me? My uncle confirmed that they would, and within a few weeks my life's direction had changed from dentistry to adventure. That was October 1951.

It would be a foolish person who refuses a lifeline, and I certainly wasn't minded to do so. I was about to take the emigrant ship, the age-old curse of our nation. Did it worry me? Not a bit. My self-confidence had come back, I was confident I could crack a simple technical course, and the path beyond was exciting. I knew that I would return.

In those years, there were no drive-on ferries. Crossings to Liverpool were by overnight steamers, which were cattle boats that also carried passengers. Upon arrival in Britain, the ship would firstly dock in Birkenhead to discharge the cattle, likely to waken sleeping passengers at an ungodly hour. It then crossed the Mersey to dock in Liverpool.

Before England implemented the 1956 Clean Air Act, the atmosphere was heavily polluted with soot and sulphurous gases. On the morning I arrived, the late September skies were sullen with low, foggy cloud and, with the heavy pollution, the atmosphere was unpleasant. As the train steamed through industrial Lancashire with its huge mills belching smoke, it was a shock – like entering Dante's *Inferno*.

Things brightened up after breakfast and a warm welcome from my uncle and aunt. My Uncle Fred was a Life Assurance salesman for the Refuge Assurance Company, an important Manchester institution. His income was modest. Aunt Rose didn't work, and they lived in a terrace house in Moston, a working-class area in North Manchester. It was an area where the proud householders whitened their doorsteps with Blanco – a practice at which I soon became adept. The only contribution I was expected to make to the housework was the Blanco job and cleaning the windows, both weekly. Manchester was so polluted with soot that it is difficult to picture it today. Every surface had a deposit of carbon; a clean shirt was needed each day. Outside features such as park benches were black with soot. Worse still, on a foggy day the atmosphere combined with the smoke creating poisonous smoky fog called smog, high in sulphur content and damaging to anyone with a bad chest. I was to experience the worst of this the following year in the Thames Estuary. After breakfast on that first morning, we went down to the Manchester wireless college in John Dalton Street, a simple place with three large lecture rooms, canteen, staff and student rooms. What excited me was the variety of electronic hardware, transmitters, receivers, direction finders and some fairly primitive radar screens. I was quickly registered and issued with the course books.

Uncle Fred bought me lunch and briefed me on transport for getting around. I was impressed to see the trolley bus system, seemingly much better than buses or trams. They ran on rubber tyres with no engine, as they were connected to an overhead electrical grid. They were noiseless with no diesel fumes and, not being confined to tracks like trams, they could glide silently up to the stop at the footpath.

We went to Piccadilly and had a look at Lewis's, the largest store in Manchester. On the way home we visited a doctor who carried out health checks on my uncle's insurance customers. As we got off the trolley bus I admired a fine display of meat in a butcher's window on the corner. 'You won't get any of that from your aunt,' my uncle told me, 'it's horsemeat.' Arriving at the surgery, my uncle introduced me to Dr Willie Reynolds and left me in the waiting room while they discussed their business. Many years later, I would meet and marry Willie's niece, Helen. I learned that he was a brother of Dr Leo Reynolds who had lived at and practiced in Scotstown. Possibly Dr Leo had ministered to my Uncle Brian when he took a bullet from the Black and Tans.

My spending money was limited, so I got a Saturday job in Lewis's store, initially working in the basement, slicing dozens of hams for the ham counter. One day they were short-staffed on the counter and asked me to help out. I preferred this as I shared in the counter commission. I loved the Manchester customers – friendly and positive. I guess they liked me too, because I was promoted full-time to the counter. I was earning a little over £1 for my day's work, quite enough to pay for my night out.

I hadn't totally reformed, and Oxford Street was the hotspot in Manchester. Many American servicemen were still stationed at a huge air base in Burton Wood. The Long Bar was a magnet to them. There was a dance hall across the road where the group was the Johnny Dankworth Seven with singer Cleo Laine. One night out per week was allowed.

A curious leftover from Victorian days were the 'Baths'. 'Are you going to the Bath tonight?' could be asking whether you were going for a swim or for a dance. Depending on the season, Victoria Baths were designed as a typical Victorian swimming pool, all white and green tiled walls. I had swum in similar baths in Tara St., Dublin, and in Belfast. When winter came, the council emptied the pool, covered it with a wooden floor, and turned it into a dance hall – unique. It worked well and had the advantage of being around the corner.

The Wireless College was great, the class size about twenty. The staff and students made me welcome. They were all natural, relaxed, nice people and we had a lot of innocent fun together. We were all serious about getting our 'ticket', our qualification, and focused on sending and reading good Morse. We had to learn the laws of radio communication, especially the use of 'Q codes' which conveyed sentences with just three letters.

Examples were QTP = "I am entering port and closing my station".

'QTC' = 'I have messages to transmit.'

'QTO' meant 'I am leaving port and opening my station,'

I quickly caught up on the course work, and was soon enjoying my progress as my Morse speed and style were coming along quite well. A curious fact about the Morse code is that one never forgets it. Seventy years later I can still read and interpret Morse code, albeit not as speedily as when I was young.

The Principal of the College was an ex-RAF radio officer, with some great stories about bomber runs over Germany (I relate some of these in Chapter 2). He recalled how once, when limping home having been battered with shrapnel from anti-aircraft fire, there was a large hole in the front window just in front of the pilot. The radio officer got the job of stuffing the hole with unwanted blankets trying to protect their boss.

The staff at the college included two lecturers who were temporarily working onshore for personal reasons but itching to get back to sea. Their anecdotes were both informative and exciting.

Soon we would qualify and take responsibility for running a solo radio operation far out to sea. We were beginning to feel just a little nervous. Our June 1952 exams were to test us to receive the Postmaster General's 'Certificate of Proficiency in Telephone and Telegraphy'. It was organised and monitored by HM Post Office, and was quite rigorous. The subjects covered included:

- accurate reception and transmission of Morse code at sixteen words per minute for ten minutes;
- workings of a transmitter and troubleshooting;
- workings of a receiver and troubleshooting;
- design and workings of emergency lifeboat transmitter;
- direction finding and echo sounding equipment;
- technical papers on lead acid batteries, charging and maintenance. International regulations on radio transmission;
- Q codes and other codes;
- radar operation and maintenance.

We all passed our examinations and I received my Certificate of Proficiency, my 'ticket', on 20 June 1952. I was into a new chapter of my life.

Armed with my new certificate, I applied for a job with the Marconi Company in their Liverpool office. There was always a demand for radio officers, so I was quickly hired and sent to the Merchant Marine office, where I was photographed, fingerprinted, and received my British Seaman's Identity Card and my Seaman's record book, both on 27 June. I was now a seaman.

The Merchant Navy is a commercial service, and not part of the armed forces. At that time, before the advent of airfreight, jumbo containerships and mammoth tankers, it was a huge network made up of many large, independent companies. All navigation and engineering officers had spent years at college and then signed contracts with one of these major shipping lines, perhaps for their entire careers. Radio was a new technology and most shipping lines were glad to subcontract the entire operation to the specialist Marconi company. This service included installation, commissioning, maintenance, and staffing of each radio station with qualified technical personnel. I was employed and paid by Marconi who would hire me out to the next available ship for the duration of the voyage. It would not be a lifetime commitment.

I now had the pleasure of getting myself kitted out with a high quality doeskin officer's uniform, complete with cuff stripes, khaki uniform, epaulettes for shoulders, and an officer's hat. As I had no money, Marconi ran an account with Silvers, the leading gentleman's outfitter in Liverpool. I bought about £50 worth of kit, underwritten by Marconi and paid for out of my salary over time.

My next adventure was an overnight train journey with three of my classmate friends. We were heading for the Marconi office in Cardiff for six weeks pre-sea training. This branch had a number of simulated radio offices where new radio officers could gain experience with different types of equipment and in different situations, sometimes problematical. We were learning new practical skills and putting into practice what we had studied.

It was June 1952 and a lovely summer to enjoy Cardiff. I was in digs with three of my friends from Manchester, relaxed and looking for recreation. Danny Kaye was performing in Llandaff Concert Hall – we snuck in through the fire door, and were allowed to stay. Cardiff docks was a well-known dangerous area, Tiger Bay, and we were warned to stay clear of it. This was, of course, an exaggeration; it was simply an area where Asian immigrants from the colonies had congregated, so it seemed alien to the Welsh. Famously, it produced the magnificent singer, Shirley Bassey.

Preparing for my first ship, I got a smallpox jab on the last day of June and wondered what sort of ship I might get. As a novice, one could work as a junior radio officer on a large ship under the guidance of a senior, or else go solo on a coastal vessel for six months to gain experience before going deep-sea. Sailing in a coaster was denigrated by deep-sea sailors, who said that, 'coastal crews were frightened when they lost sight of land,' to which the inshore sailors replied, 'like the way deep-sea crews feel when they catch sight of land.'

Which would I be selected for? I hadn't long to wait.

CHAPTER 4

ALIVE ON THE OCEAN WAVE

EARLIER THAT DAY WE had been facing a southwesterly, driving into the seas, rocking up and down fore to aft, bow either burrowing into the huge waves or rising up, up, up, to the top of the waves, the ship climbing to an angle of 25–30 degrees before banging down into the trough with a spine-juddering crash, every part of the ship creaking and groaning, uncomfortable and awful, yes, but now we come to Land's End. Quietly, new orders to the helmsman: 'Bring us round to 285 degrees.'

Later the wind had freshened to gale force seven and rising. We were heading up towards the Bristol Channel and with no shelter on that stretch, we had to tie everything down and hold on tight. The ship came round to 360 degrees, heading due North. We had now exposed our entire port beam to the weather.

For the next two hours the ship rolled in a crazy rocking motion as the waves pushed us over to a dangerous angle. We hoped it would stop before we rolled upside down.

There was an inclinometer fixed on the forward bulkhead in the bridge, a pendulum pointing down to an ark marked in degrees. There were two red marks on the gauge, one on the port and one on the starboard side: the angles of no return. We kept an anxious eye on it as we hung on grimly, bracing our feet widely to retain some balance.

The pendulum swung wider, getting closer to the red mark. At last, a new order: 'Come round to forty-five degrees.' Slowly, the ship turned into the new course, with the seas behind us, the rolling gone. The tension started to ease, and the steward appeared with mugs of cocoa.

And I thought, 'What is a young man from an inland town in Ireland doing risking his life on one of the worst seas on earth?'

In uniform for a friend's wedding

Growing up in Monaghan town in the late 1930s and early 1940s, the idea of a sea with mighty waves could well have been a myth, like living in Oklahoma. Indeed, I was ten years old, on holidays in Bundoran in 1943, when I first heard the roar of the seas.

I was to make up for that during the next two years.

After six weeks training in the Cardiff Marconi Centre I was handed two items. One was a cheque for my very first month's salary – very welcome. Even nicer was a commission to travel on the following Friday to Newcastle-upon-Tyne to take up the position of First Radio Officer aboard M.V. *Dame Caroline Hazlett*, a coaster. I was to take up duty on Sunday, ready to sail on the Monday.

As the taxi brought me to the designated address, I thought, *This isn't the docks.* It was a power station, with no sign of a ship. The power station staff knew otherwise, and directed the taxi towards the river. There she was, covered in coal dust; what looked to me like a barge, no funnel, and no mast. Was this a sea-going ship?

Named after Dame Caroline Hazlett, the wife of a previous Chairman of the National Coal Board, this was a new coastal collier designed to carry coal from South Wales and Newcastle direct to the London power stations at Battersea and Fulham. I would learn that although small, at two thousand tons, it was extremely powerful and well fitted-out. I had a comfortable cabin with an en suite bathroom. The radio office was fitted with the very latest gear. This would be my home for the next six months.

Captain Richmond examined my papers and welcomed me aboard. I signed the ship's articles and was registered as a member of the crew on 13 August 1952. The small crew consisted of six officers and about eight seamen. The officers were the Captain (Welsh); First Mate (or First Officer), also Welsh;

the Second Mate (Cockney); Chief Engineer (Welsh); Second Engineer (English); and me. The crew of six able seamen were led by the Bo'sun (from Wexford), assisted by the 'Lampie'; this name derives from Lamp Trimmer, in the paraffin lamp era. We had one cook/steward to look after us. The second mate, aged about twenty-two, was very friendly to me and taught me much. An ex-Royal Navy seaman, he told me how, during and soon after the war, many skilled yachtsmen had joined as Royal Naval Volunteer Reserves (RNVR), referred to sarcastically by professional officers as 'gentlemen trying to be sailors'; to which they replied, 'like you sailors trying to be gentlemen'!

The ship's itinerary was highly repetitive: one week's round trip to Barry Docks, near Cardiff, and the next week to Newcastle. In each case, it was back to London, either to Fulham or Battersea. As we were never more than one week away from home port, we only carried provisions for ten days, no shop, and sadly no duty free.

The officers were a fairly rough lot, but I quickly settled in and began to enjoy what was an eye-opening and very exciting time. To be paid for cruising in comfort – fabulous!

We put to sea on a glorious August day and I opened up my radio station for the very first time with the call sign *GDTR: QTO* (leaving port) *QTC500* (am listening on 500 kilocycles). By the use of Q codes and plain text, every ship keeps the nearest coastal radio station informed about their location, where they're headed, and which radio station the ship is signing on or off to listen to.

As we sailed around the coast, I would sign off one station and sign on to the next: Newcastle (GCC), Humber (GKZ), North Foreland (GNF), Isle of White (GNI), Landsend (GLD), Anglesea (GLV). This was necessary for safety at sea and for the owners to contact and direct the ship's Captain if necessary.

Every marine radio station listens on the medium wave international calling frequency of 500 kilocycles and uses it to call other stations and to be called on. 500 kcs is a busy and emergency channel so it can only be used briefly to call up and then switch to another frequency 512, 530, 498, for the necessary communications.

Once every half hour all radio traffic ceases for three minutes, 0015–0018 and 0045–0048, and all listen in silence in case someone is in distress and signalling for help. I was to hear many such calls over the next two years.

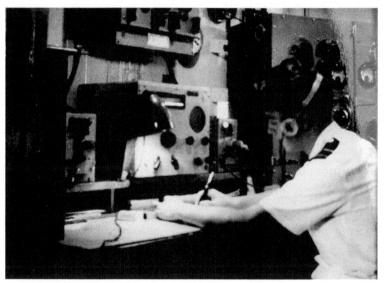

My marine radio station

My first two days at sea were exciting as I watched out for the various headlands with powerful ship's binoculars. It was like cruising in a big yacht. All navigating officers like to talk navigation, so we studied the charts in the chart room and I tried to figure out where we were.

On the third morning as we turned into the Thames estuary, we started to prepare the ship for its voyage up river to Fulham.

The brilliant design that enabled our two thousand-ton cargo ship to sail under the London bridges required us to adopt a low profile – literally. As we sailed past Southend, I closed the radio station, switched off all transmitter power and so informed the captain. Lower the masts. As the masts slowly telescoped downwards, I was on top of the cargo hold cover with two seamen manhandling the aerial gear to protect it from damage as it was slowly lowered, guiding it on to the deck away from the hold covers which would soon be opened to discharge their coal.

My transmitting gear included about 230-foot lengths of copper aerials (main and emergency) together with breakable earthenware insulating cups. A kink in the aerial wire would cause it to snap when it came under tension with potentially serious consequences.

That done, and on with a reefer jacket and up to the fo'castle to join the Cockney second mate for a conducted marine tour of London's great port. I had never been to London before, whereas the mate loved it as his hometown. I couldn't have had a more devoted introduction.

It was early on a glorious August morning, and the mate explained every detail of the passing shoreline, the great marine buildings, the gigantic docks, and of course the bridges. It was a scene I was to see often in the coming months and although I never tired of it, that first morning is still bright in my mind.

At that time, London was one of the world's great ports for freight and for passengers. As our small barge-like vessel moved quietly upstream, we passed many great carriers from all corners of the globe, some with household names,: Union Castle, P & O, Ellermans, Holland America, Cunard, Moore McCormack; some anchored, waiting for docking space, some departing, some moving more slowly than us because of their great size.

I learned that our captain and first mate were qualified to bring the ship to dock without a pilot and could be relied on to make good time, especially if it was getting near to pub closing time.

The next six months passed quickly. Mostly it was rather monotonous, forwards and backwards, South Wales to London to South Shields – a miserable little port near Newcastle. The months of September and October were mostly bright and sunny and I did a lot of sunbathing on the deck during my off-duty periods.

The ship was fitted with a Decca Navigating System, which enabled the navigation officer to plot the position. For recreation I would compete with the mates in using my own Direction-Finding Radio and a remote global system called Loran. They were not best pleased that a young cub just out of school could match their traditional skills, for which they had studied and sat in exam halls for years.

As autumn faded away the weather began to deteriorate, and we hunkered down for a winter of some of the worst weather on earth. Land's End is notoriously exposed to the North Atlantic storms and as we rounded the peninsula we turned broadside on to the mighty seas. We saw some frightful weather and may have been lucky once or twice not to have come to some harm.

Was I ever frightened? Not really, but often very concerned.

There were frequent gales, some storm force eight with occasional gusts up to force ten, storm force, and even force eleven, violent storm! As most of our weather is from the west we suffered most while sailing empty on the voyages from London to South Wales. When we were fully loaded, we were very low in the water with a low centre of gravity, making us fairly stable. But when we were 'light ship', we stood high out of the water, and with a flat-bottomed hull we were easy prey to a heavy sea and a storm force wind.

A complication in managing our west-bound voyages was that the captain, mate and chief engineer lived in South Wales. The desire to bring the ship to Barry docks in time for the weekend was a constant influence on how long we would shelter en route.

All through the next three months we took everything that the North Atlantic could throw at us. Hugging the coast and totally concentrated on weather forecasts, we punched our way through every kind of storm to keep supplies flowing to the London power stations, which were now consuming vast quantities of coal. As gales could last for two or three days we couldn't shelter for long and we battled through force seven touching force eight many times. Imagine great, forty-foot white rollers towering, crashing down on the decks, completely submerging us like a submarine. There were huge waves roaring up the deck and beating on the glass windows of the wheel house, a world of white water, zero visibility, and hammering, hammering, hammering for hour after hour. With headaches and empty stomachs we just had to take it – no alternative.

Every so often we could take no more or the weather was worsening and the question was where to shelter. My radio office opened directly off the bridge/wheelhouse so I was totally party to all the discussions, arguments and occasional disagreements. As I was continually feeding in the latest weather (WX) reports from coastal stations many miles ahead of us, I could bring an update every ten or fifteen minutes. If the gale was north-westerly we had a choice of bays, as the landmass of England would help protect us. We could therefore stop off every fifty miles or so. But when the south-westerly gales hit us shelter was more uncertain as most bays only offered part shelter. This provoked a debate: Weather is very bad and getting worse by the hour. Do we run for the nearest shelter where we may be driven ashore on the rocks or do we battle on for another fifty miles (five hours) to reach full shelter? Better shelter from south-westerly was at the Isle of Wight, Bournemouth (four hours) Portland Bill (three hours), Torbay (five hours), St Austell (eight hours), Falmouth (three hours) and Penzance (five hours). The most exposed section under a S.W. gale was from Torbay to Falmouth, about nine to ten hours sailing. Finally, we needed to use Penzance Bay to eat some sustenance and grab a few hours' sleep before the worst bit – rounding Land's End, the nightmare I described earlier.

Slowly the ship came round and the tension started to relax. We could all breathe again. The sea was now following us, pushing us ahead; a new waggling motion and another roller coaster, but not as bad. Another fifteen hours and we'd be getting into port. Miserable little Barry town would look very good.

But what happened if it was a north-westerly? No problem, as we sail along the south coast. Unpleasant, but no danger. Then we would get to Penzance bay and need to have a think. There is no fully sheltered bay on the west coast of Cornwall or Devon, almost a hundred miles of exposed coastline with one of the worst seas on earth, ten to twelve hours of danger. This is when the officers would think of a weekend at home and it twisted their thinking a little.

One voyage we decided to go around Cape Cornwall into the teeth of a force seven. We looked into St. Ives bay for a few hours but it was no haven. Better to press on, relying on our powerful engine. Around mid-morning the radar showed a ship overtaking us. In the mucky white haze of the storm we watched as HMS *Wave*, a powerful Royal Navy Fisheries Protection Frigate, passed us at speed

The wind freshened to gale force eight and rising. It was time to look for shelter. We dropped two anchors in Constantine Bay and tucked in under Trevose Head, our engines running in case we needed to stand off in a hurry. HMS *Wave* was also anchored there, but further out from the land and more exposed. We settled down to wait out the worst of the storm. It was early afternoon when I heard a shout from the officer of the watch, the second mate, 'The crazy bugger is going out.' We watched in some surprise and doubt. If he thought it was safe, why not us? Should we go for it? If it had been a Friday, who knows? Anyway, we stayed in shelter through the night. By morning, the storm had abated and we headed out into the still-rough seas.

Later that day we heard on the BBC that Royal Naval vessel HMS *Wave* had been driven ashore on the Cornish coast and was a complete wreck. Thankfully no lives were lost, but I learned later that the commander had been discharged.

One Friday we found ourselves in a similar situation. The weather was awful, with a force seven from the northwest giving us a very bad time; we were beating up the coast with the weather hitting us hard full on the port bow, and all of us sick and tired. Came the discussion about shelter, the wind had freshened to force eight, a full gale, and the glass was still dropping – would we seek shelter or plough on? Captains are supposed to make all decisions, but in the intimacy of a small group of officers it was usual to talk about the weather, and of course both navigation officers had to manage the ship during their watch. Anyway, we had a real dispute. This was the nearest thing to a mutiny that I experienced. The captain, Welsh first officer, and chief engineer all wanted to brave it out and sail through the night to reach Barry on Saturday morning. The second officer, second engineer, and I felt that we would be risking the safety of the ship and our lives. To turn into the Bristol Channel, heading for Barry on a bearing of forty-five degrees, going round to nearly ninety degrees, would expose our length to the full force of the gale, which looked like it might freshen further into a storm. Being 'light ship', we were well out of the water. I had seen the pendulum of no return swing dangerously close to the red zone and I honestly thought that we might be turned over or driven on to the headland.

Finally, it was agreed to keep on a safer bearing straight north up to Lundy Island. We would reach Lundy about 10.00 p.m., shelter there for the night, and review the situation at daybreak. By 5.00 a.m., the wind had dropped to about force five and while the seas were still running high it was decided to make a run for it. As we came out from Lundy on a bearing of seventy degrees, we suffered the onslaught of huge waves on to our entire port length pushing us sideways towards the Cornish coast, threatening to turn us over. But the wind had softened and our little ship could resist the force of the waves.

We reached port mid-morning and our Welsh shipmates were home for lunch.

To convey some idea of the seas we sailed through, one morning after a storm I saw a metal ladder that had been clamped to an outside bulkhead had two steel clamps broken off and the ladder had been bent back into a u-shape.

It wasn't always stormy. There were many pleasant, uneventful days when it was a pleasure to be at sea. Endless conversations and stories enlivened by the occasional glimpse of another vessel, sometimes a big one.

As the autumn mists drew in, this created another hazard. I remember days when I couldn't see the other side of the bridge, let alone the bow. The use of our powerful radar made life safer. There was no GPS in those days, but my direction finder equipment could give me two, sometimes three, cross bearings, which with the echo sounder enabled me to plot our position. When I provided this to the Officer of the Watch,

I was required to qualify its accuracy, one to five. In close proximity to coastal stations with no static electricity and no radio interference, these were usually grade one. Also, from the daily reading of the trailing 'log', the navigators knew the distance travelled plus their bearing, so they could calculate a 'dead reckoning'. Between us, we could manage our normal ten knots in zero visibility.

Fog at sea was clean and white, but when we approached port things changed. The droplets of moisture in the fog would mix with the soot particles of factory and domestic smoke to form 'smog.' Since the Clean Air Act of 1956 has improved conditions, it is almost impossible to understand how bad this smog was; not only filthy dirty, but a killer to people with bad chests. For over a century, the legislators and pressure groups such as the Smoke Abatement League had been seeking some control on the use of coal in domestic fires and industrial boilers, but no action had been taken.

Then one December it all came together in what became known as 'The Great Smog' of 1952. Sailing south from the Tyne, we were aware from weather forecasts and the BBC that an unusual situation was developing, but nothing prepared us for the unforgettable experience of the next week.

We had been slowed by banks of fog all down the east coast and were running late as we approached the Thames estuary from the north. It was Friday 5 December, the crew were on full alert, but with our excellent radar we were in little danger. Our radar could focus on a ten-mile radius or a twenty-five-mile radius. I had been on the local range, but switched to the wider range to watch for increasing traffic from the south and east.

At first, I didn't understand what I was looking at, almost like the snowy picture seen on early TVs with a poor signal. It was more like number of blips. What was happening? Was the set faulty? The entire estuary above Southend was showing a great number of objects – hundreds – all in our path. All stationary. Outside, the fog was getting denser and although it was daylight we could barely see beyond the bow.

Stopping our engine, we slowed down. There was no wind and we gradually became stationary. I had not yet closed the radio station so I made a quick call to 'CQ' – all stations QSL 512 'I am working on 512.' I quickly sent out a message, 'What's happening?' About ten ships answered: 'The port is closed; the pilots won't take us in.' The blips on my radar were ships anchored in the estuary, hundreds of them.

Unbelievable!

With engine restarted we edged further into the estuary and dropped our anchor roughly opposite Southend-on-Sea, cocooned in a dense shroud of impenetrable fog – not yet smog, still white and normal.

For the next twenty-four hours we rested and listened. The BBC announced that a serious weather condition was developing in the city and advised everyone to stay indoors as much as possible. People with bad chests were warned not to risk going outside. What was happening? The weather in late November and early December had been considerably colder than average and the people of London were burning large quantities of coal.

What started off as a normal fog turned very dangerous where the fog became trapped beneath the temperature inversion of an anti-cyclone. A layer of fog one to two hundred metres deep absorbed the soot particles and gases emitted from factory chimneys and thousands of household grates. Visibility dropped to a few metres. In many parts of London, as I was to discover, it was impossible, at night, for pedestrians to find their way, even in familiar streets. In the Isle of Dogs, the visibility was, at times, nil. People couldn't see their own feet. At Heathrow Airport visibility remained below ten metres for forty-eight hours on the 6 and 7 December.

Throughout that week, huge quantities of pollutants continued to be emitted every day as people tried to keep warm, thousands of tons of soot, of carbon dioxide, of hydrochloric acid, of fluorine and most dangerous of all, sulphur dioxide, which in the wet air converted into sulphuric acid. The concentration of smoke increased from .49 mgs per cubic metre on 4 December to 4.46 on the 7th and 8th.

The effects of the smog were shocking, causing premature death to thousands and inconvenience to millions. Mortality from bronchitis and pneumonia increased more than sevenfold, killing an estimated four thousand people. Road, marine, rail, and air traffic was brought almost to a standstill. Cattle at Smithfield Market were asphyxiated. Incredibly, a performance at the Saddler's Well theatre had to be suspended, when fog in the auditorium reduced visibility to the point when the performers couldn't be seen.

Meanwhile, we were wondering what to do. As a coaster, we only carried limited provisions. We could hear the sounds from Southend through the still white curtain. Fresh milk and bread would be welcome. The first officer was detailed to fetch provisions using one of the lifeboats. I had kept the radio station on air and we asked for directions from our British Coal control. The cold weather had increased demand for electricity and Battersea fuel supplies were running low. It was the captain's decision, but if we could deliver, it would be appreciated.

The next part of our voyage was magical as we slowly waltzed up the estuary through hundreds of towering cruisers. While there were many ships parked between us and our destination, the distance between them was considerable and we were relatively small. With three men on the bow, me on radar, and every man listening, we inched our way upstream past many of the great liners of the day. Each of the anchored ships had a man ringing the ships bell every twenty or thirty seconds.

Apart from the low dull throb of our engine, and the bells, there was an uncanny silence. Nudging our way forward, the lonely bells directed us to avoid the huge sterns of ocean-going liners. Sometimes only thirty feet separated us from a collision as we corrected course – gingerly, so as to avoid another ship on the other side. In all we counted over a hundred ships as we tiptoed past making less than one knot.

It says a lot for the captain and crew that we achieved this extraordinary feat – the only ship to enter the Port of London in several days. As we got closer to London, our navigation became easier and soon we had the Thames estuary to ourselves as we exited the 'parking' zone and met no other vessel. However, the fog was getting denser and darker, changing from the white cotton wool to a yellow, viscous-coloured curtain that reduced visibility even further. The next problem was to navigate the bridges and actually find Battersea Power Station.

Finally, our epic voyage ended and the vigilance of our crew was rewarded as we docked safely with two thousand tons of eagerly-awaited coal to keep London's lights shining.

At that time my sister Maura was working in London, and I had agreed to have dinner with her and stay the night in her apartment in Ealing. The Underground was still functioning and I soon reached Ealing station. However, I then needed to cross Ealing Common, but I couldn't see the edge of the footpath. I joined a small group who were clustered around a policeman carrying a large, blazing pitch torch. We all held hands and stayed very close as we were led across the large Common. At the other end, I felt my way along the railings peering into the gloom. I was glad to arrive at Maura's apartment and to warm myself before a blazing coal fire. I had survived the Great Smog of London!

Four years later, the Clean Air Act was passed in 1956.

Earlier I mentioned the two periods of radio silence when we all listened out for distress calls. During my months on the coast I had many occasions to listen to the dreaded SOS as some poor ship found itself in trouble. None were near me so that, thankfully, I was never directly involved.

On the morning of Saturday 31 January 1953, we were anchored in Penzance Bay sheltering from yet another storm, when I opened up the radio station and went on watch. It was 8.00 a.m., but there was no sound of ships' radio traffic – just silence. I checked to ensure my radio was working, and waited. Then I heard another ship leaving port calling QTO to his nearest coastal station. There was a short, sharp reprimand from the coast station: an emergency was in place, use 512, maintain silence on 500.

The picture slowly emerged. The Radio Officer (RO) of the car ferry *Princess Victoria* was calling for help. The ship was in distress in the Irish Sea just outside Stranraer. Hundreds of R.O.'s all around these waters would be listening and we all held our breath as the situation developed. About three ships responded that they were in the neighbourhood – 'exact position, please.' Just then, a Royal Navy Destroyer, H.M.S. *Contest*, opened up and took control.

I should explain that the Royal and other fighting navies have their own operating wavebands and do not normally communicate on the merchant wavebands. Usually the merchant ship nearest to the distressed vessel controls the sequence of radio transmissions, but if a Royal Navy vessel is close by, it is authorised to take control. A destroyer can move at up to 32/35 knots while a merchant ship is more likely to have a top speed of 10/14 knots.

There followed a number of heart-rending transmissions. As per marine regulations, I wrote down every communication in my radio log, which is an official document to be returned via the Marconi Company to the UK Ministry of Marine at the end of each trip.

The first call for help at 9.46 was an *XXX* indicating an urgent rather than an emergency situation. This didn't fully reflect the dire position, and it wasn't until 10.43 that the first SOS was sent. HMS *Contest* computed the ETA of the nearest ships to the *Victoria*, but none were near enough to offer assistance. As the minutes, then hours, passed, the ship was listing heavily and taking water rapidly until we heard that the order to abandon ship had been given but that the RO would stay on duty. HMS *Contest* said they'd be on site in an hour and a half. *Victoria* thanked *Contest* and said he would wait.

In all, RO David Broadfoot transmitted over fifty messages during the six hours that the ship struggled to survive, finally standing on the beam rather than on the deck as the ship listed to seventy degrees with water flowing into the radio cabin. Still sending out the estimated position, he sent, 'Sorry for the Morse quality, on beam end.' After a period of silence, the *Victoria* called to say that the ship was going down, the list was over eighty degrees, and it would roll over any minute. At 13.58 he was still transmitting, when his radio fell silent. The *Contest* called and called, but there was only silence.

The ship was gone and a very brave RO with it.

I found that I was crying, as were several other officers who had crowded into the radio office to follow the drama. Radio Officer Broadfoot was posthumously awarded the George Cross.

The tragedy had been almost inevitable when the ferry put to sea into the path of a gale Force 8, strengthening to Storm Force 10/11. The waves would have been over forty-five feet with winds gusting up to sixty knots. The ship had barely left the shelter of Stranraer's Loch Ryan when it was struck by a massive wave, which crashed over the open car deck and burst open the stern doors. The cargo broke loose and fell to the starboard side, blocking the already inadequate scuppers and preventing the invading seawater from escaping. With the scuppers blocked and the stern doors open to the mountainous waves the ship began to list heavily and it was only a matter of time.

Loss of life was 134, including the captain and all the ship's officers. There were forty-four survivors, none of them women or children.

Quite the saddest day of my time at sea.

I was now approaching the end of my six-month contract, and when we arrived in South Wales, I visited the Marconi office in Cardiff to enquire about my next posting. We had previously discussed it and the local manager thought I would get a deep-sea appointment. Captain Richmond knew that we would head north to the Tyne on our next two voyages. Marconi would access their database seeking to match my movements with their requirements.

On 8 February I signed off the *Dame Caroline Hazlett* in Newcastle. When I reported to the Marconi Office in Newcastle, I was told to stay overnight in the Officers' Club as they had a ship for me.

The next day, I was instructed to join MV *Norrisia*, an ocean-going Shell Oil tanker bound for the Caribbean – good news on a bleak February day on the North Sea. The *Norrisia* (call sign GBPJ) was registered at eight thousand tons, and when I joined her at Tyne Piers in Jarrow she was 'light ship', i.e. unloaded, and she looked as big as a castle. I was moving up in the world and it was exciting.

I signed on the Ship's Articles on 10 February and began to familiarise myself with my new gear. This was designed for high frequency transmissions using the earth ionosphere (the Heaviside Layers) for long distance communications over thousands of miles. It was my first experience of this gear but I was well qualified and competent to handle it.

Having said that, I was disappointed some two weeks later when I first transmitted on H.F. I didn't have the power I expected, but I struggled on for some days before I undertook some serious remedial investigations. I found a dead mouse totally carbonised, lying across the output terminals at the rear of the main transmitter. The carcass was causing a partial short circuit of power, sufficient to reduce my transmission power but not enough to short out the entire operation. A mouse with bad timing.

Marconi had arranged for a Mr Ibbs to carry out a routine maintenance visit on the 12th so I had the 11th to visit the marine outfitters in Newcastle to fit myself out with tropical gear: khaki for working hours and white gear for off duty in the tropics, plus white covers for my hat. It cost £39, quite a lot in 1953.

On 12 February I worked with Mr Ibbs who gave me lots of insights into the radio equipment, a useful tutorial.

On 13 February, we slipped our moorings and headed out into the cold grey North Sea headed for the sun. I opened up my station: 'GCC....GBPJ (us)...QTO Newcastle bnd Curacao via Rotterdam, Las Palmas.'

The *Norrisia* was named after a seashell, as are all the ships in the Shell fleet, respecting the origins of the Shell Company. The Solomon brothers had started the Shell business in South East Asia, shipping trinket boxes decorated with shells as novelties to London. They had become known as the Shell Company well before they started a trade shipping barrels of lamp oil and paraffin oil from Indonesia to Europe. The oil trade quickly superseded the trinket boxes and Shell Petroleum was born.

All tankers carry their cargo below sea level so that their decks are spacious with no need for hold covers, derricks, and cranes. This allows lots of room for accommodation and as tanker voyages tend to be long, the owners compensate by providing spacious accommodation. I hadn't known this before and was delighted to find myself in a spacious suite. I was also to find that the standard of food was extremely high for the same reason.

The ship's master was Captain Green, a pleasant, authoritative man who controlled his ship in a quiet manner. He made me welcome and was inclined to treat me in a fatherly manner; I was only aged nineteen and he later advised me from time to time on how I should not stay too long in a maritime career. Newly-arrived into a very attractive and exciting job, it wasn't advice I wanted to hear, but he was right.

As soon as we cleared the three-mile line, the chief steward opened up the bond and invited orders. I bought DeKuypers gin at twenty pence per bottle, as there was no UK brand. Joining my new shipmates over a few drinks I slowly realised that I was going to be sick. After six months in rough waters, I thought I could take anything; however, I was used to the short pitch and roll of a small ship. This was a completely different motion, and it got to me. My memory associated the gin with the discomfort and for some years afterwards I didn't like the smell of gin and couldn't drink it. Happily, I got over that in time.

Our first port of call was Rotterdam to load with high-octane fuel destined for Las Palmas in the Canary Islands. With Dutch efficiency we were quickly loaded overnight, while I slept and didn't get ashore.

The following was my first day at sea and I joined three junior officers at table for breakfast. Having grown up in a middle class home, I was comfortable with table settings and etiquette, which was as well as things were quite formal. The stewards were everywhere, ready to take one's order and serve. Breakfast was a real treat with a wide choice of tropical fruits, juices, and kedgeree, which I had never previously seen. I was to find that the cuisine on the Norrisia reflected the ship's return from the tropics with a wide range of foodstuff preserved in the ship's refrigerators. England was still recovering from a world war, and local supplies were still limited.

The first challenge in the dining room at dinner was to how to tackle Asparagus au Beurre Noir. I was okay with the French but had never heard of white asparagus. This was a long way from boarding school in wartime. It would take some years before I realised that not all asparagus is white. I later learned that the ship's cook had served all over the world and was particularly fond of Dutch Indonesian cuisine. I was soon introduced to Nasi Goreng, Satay, Rijsttafel (rice table), and Indonesian curry.

Las Palmas was interesting. This was long before the days of mass tourism and the places I was to see were totally unspoilt. I visited Las Palmas on almost every voyage. It was on the way to and from almost everywhere. On the outward journey we would always stop – even if we had nothing to discharge – to top up with fresh water. There is a folk memory, almost a neurosis in the Merchant Navy about fresh water, probably dating from the days of sail when water in the doldrums was life and death. Our ships never missed an opportunity to top up their water supplies even on short voyages.

1953 was long before the arrival of the mammoth tankers of the sixties and seventies. The newer vessels were then being launched at up to twenty thousand tons and with high efficiency pumps could discharge their cargoes in twelve hours, and then back out to sea again. The *Norrisia* was an old ship and its pumps were slow and inefficient. Great! This meant that it could take two days to unload us, which gave me time ashore. A radio officer could carry out all necessary maintenance while at sea, and with no duties aboard, I was off duty from closing down the station (QTP) until I opened it up on departure (QTO). All other officers have some duties while in port, and I was the object of some gentle resentment – nothing personal – just ROs in general.

I wandered up to the Catholic Church on that first Sunday morning and was spotted by the parish priest, who, clearly intrigued by this foreigner, invited me to serve Mass. It was all in Latin in those days. He had no English and I had no Spanish, but a few Latin words and some body language helped.

That afternoon I took a bus ride around the entire island. Stopping at a taverna for refreshments, I stumbled into a small wedding celebration and again was made welcome. On the following day, four of us went to the beach for a swim. Changing into our swimming togs as we would at home, we were spotted by the police who were very cross about such indecency. Reluctantly, we paid for a beach hut. How times have changed in fifty years.

Our next destination was Curacao in the Dutch West Indies to load high-octane fuel for Havana, Cuba.

Sailing in the mid-Atlantic is lovely – very peaceful with a slow swell, nothing to see from horizon to horizon and usually good weather. Throughout my deep-sea voyages I never experienced bad weather in the Atlantic – only in the Bay of Biscay and very occasionally in the West Indies.

We were now in our tropical white uniforms, having crossed the equator. At twelve knots we covered nearly three hundred miles per twenty-four hours. Going west we turned the clock back every few days. I continued to keep my watch in four sessions of two hours each: 8.00–10.00 a.m., 12.00 noon–2.00 p.m., 4.00–6.00 p.m., and 8.00–10.00 p.m. I observed the silence periods on 500 cycles medium wave while also tuning in on high frequency to listen for calls on the 6, 8, or 10 kilocycle bands. Tables advised me on which H.F. bands to use around the globe depending on seasons and local WX conditions.

One of my duties in the Safety at Sea mode was to charge and carefully maintain two large banks of batteries. These were never normally used but would always be available to power my transmitter in the event of a breakdown in the ship's power system, i.e. in distress.

We arrived at Willemstad, the capital of Curacao, at 8.00 a.m. and held up the rush hour traffic as a swing bridge opened to let us into port. Our second steward was dumping the break-fast leftovers at the stern causing a frenzy of shark activity – I counted about nine of them. Willemstad was boring, with little to commend it. It was very hot and I enjoyed swimming at the Shell club in spite of having my money stolen while in the pool.

The Dutch Antilles consists of three volcanic rocky islands: Curacao, Aruba, and Bonaire. A relic of imperial aspirations, they seemed useless until a sea of oil was discovered in Vene-zuela. The Royal Dutch Shell Company built oil refineries on Aruba and Curacao and imported Dutch citizens to run them.

Again with Dutch pragmatism, they protected their expatri-ate wives' virtue by establishing 'Camp Allegre', also known as Happy Valley. They recruited women from other West Indian islands and imported them for a two-year contract as prostitutes to let them earn their dowry.

From Curacao, we sailed to Havana and tied up near to the old fort at the harbour entrance. We managed three days there because our pumps couldn't pump our cargo up to tanks on a hilltop. After three days someone noticed the wheeze and brought down a powerful pump that emptied us in twelve hours. Pity!

Havana was my first experience of an old Spanish city. It was throbbing with life, music and dancing everywhere. I caught a taxi to a recommended beach and was shocked at a charge of $1 to enter. Quite a lot in 1953. It was worth it, with a restaurant, rumba dance band, boardwalk, and dance floor and of course the beach. This was the first time I danced in the afternoon only wearing swimming costumes. Cool. The Shell Club in Havana had a nightclub, which was fun for a young, single sailor.

One of the advantages of sailing with an experienced shipping company, the old hands knew all the scams, when and where to sell cigarettes and what currency would fetch a good return. For example, there was a shortage of American cigarettes in Havana. I remember selling a carton of Lucky Strikes to a local in a two-room shack with a 24" TV set. He paid me $3 for the cigarettes, which had cost me 10p. We then sailed to Venezuela where dollars were in great demand. I sold the dollars for three times their value, which gave me enough spending money for the visit, plus a couple of Arrow shirts and a shark skin hat!

The self-funding by selling cigarettes and money was repeated on nearly every trip. Also my shipmates knew the ropes, knew good bars, safe parts of town what you could and could not do. It gave me a fast track to the situation, a little bit like a good tour guide.

Venezuela was a huge producer of oil. The port is inland through a short bottleneck and about thirty to fifty miles of an almost inland lake, sailing between the nodding donkey pumps, the lake of Maracaibo, a lake of oil right on the equator in April; very, very hot.

We brought a load of crude to Curacao and were then ordered light ship to the Persian Gulf via Suez. We'd been at sea for about two weeks, just south of Italy, when London discovered their outrageous mistake: that we wouldn't be allowed through the Canal because we had previously called on Haifa in Israel. There was no alternative but to spend a further two weeks sailing back to Curacao where we loaded with high-octane petrol for England. I arrived back in Birkenhead on 12 June after a four-month adventure. They were paying me for something I would have done for free.

The pay was good. For every weekend out of the UK we were paid for two extra days for Sundays, and one extra day for Saturdays – i.e. three days every seven days, also double for Bank Holidays; in this case, four days for Easter. This amounted to forty-three extra days pay on a ninety-one-day voyage. Good money for a twenty-year-old. Also, our accommodation was inclusive of everything except drinks and cigarettes. With gin at 20p and cigs at 10p, plus various little scams or black market, one could see the bank balance climbing rapidly.

After a brief holiday, visiting Uncle Fred in Manchester and Mum in Monaghan, I was back in Liverpool.

One of that city's oldest home-grown shipping firms was T & J Harrison (Hungry Harrison) who ran about fourteen ships all with names of occupations, for example, the *Adviser*, the *Linguist* etc. I sailed on the *Adviser* on 30 June to Barbados and various other West Indian islands, then down to Georgetown, British Guiana. It was a great trip. My fellow officers were mostly Liverpudlians under an Irish Captain Penston. In my experience, the people of Liverpool have more fun than most other English. The crew were West Indian. The assistant steward was Colin Jones, a very affable young man with a café au lait complexion. Harrison had serviced Barbados for generations, and we were almost family in Barbados. Two of Colin's brothers, Winthrop and Justin, were also stewards on Harrison ships. This was a very pleasant and enjoyable voyage.

We picked up a temporary steward in Barbados whose usual job was cocktail barman at the Barbados Racetrack. He spoiled us with the best Planter's Punch I have ever tasted.

With a feisty young gang of officers, it was inevitable that we occasionally had a little too much to drink – this might get us into scrapes from time to time.

One night, four of us were in a bar in Port of Spain, Trinidad, and met up against some Marines who were teasing us as 'f★★★★★ Limeys'. Things got a little hot, and then we all got involved with a local crowd who didn't like Americans or English. When bottles started flying, the situation was getting serious and we were relieved to see two US Marine Guards arrive with three-foot-long batons ready to break heads if necessary. As they rounded up the Americans we welcomed them and started to join them. 'Are you guys American? No? Then f★★★ off.' We legged it out of there pretty quickly.

Rum was much stronger there than in Europe, and unbelievably cheap. When six of us went into a bar and each put a dollar in the kitty, it bought a bottle of rum and six cokes for five dollars and left a dollar over, so that after five rounds there were five dollars over to buy an extra round.

Last man standing ordered the taxi!

I got worried one night as we sailed down to British Guiana. The electronic static was crashing in my ears, as I tried to get reliable signals to establish a location with my direction finder. I could not define the location of any signals due to the static. We were sailing in an area where there were many rocks and small islands and we needed to know precisely where we were. The night was blowing a nasty squall, it was pitch dark, and visibility was very poor. The deck officers couldn't get a fix on anything other than a 'dead reckoning', based on bearing and distance travelled. This makes no allowance for tidal drift or wind effect and at best is only an approximation.

The Captain kept asking me for a radio fix, but the best I could do was quality five, which means unreliable and poor quality. He wasn't happy about this and I hung around on the bridge until 1.00 or 2.00 a.m. still trying, but without success. I wondered why he didn't slow down and wait until dawn, when he would have visibility and the static would have died away, allowing me to get some quality into my position reporting.

I slept for about three hours and was up before dawn and kept at it as the static slowly diminished and I could focus on the distant signals. At last I had a quality two position; a big relief for the skipper and me.

While I privately questioned the skipper's judgement in sailing at top speed on an ill-defined route, I knew that he had a very difficult mandate. It costs a lot to keep a fully-manned ship at sea and the owners expect delivery on time. No doubt it was this that drove the skipper. The sad fact is that this man, Captain Penston, did in fact lose his ship on the next voyage. I never heard the details other than there were no deaths, but he was sacked.

Returning to Liverpool on 8 September after two months of fun I worked on the *Linguist* for two weeks as it sailed to Bristol for minor repairs, then back again to Liverpool where I was to begin what was to be my last and nicest voyage.

The South American Saint Line – all of the ships were called after saints – operated a regular service carrying cargo and on some of their ships up to twelve passengers. Competing with the market leader Royal Mail Liners, it positioned itself as the poor man's Rolls Royce. Passengers were typically children of expatriate managers travelling to school in England. As such, it sought to employ officers from public schools who would present the right image. One of my fellow officers had been to Rugby and another was the son of a colonel in the Indian Army.

I joined the *St. Merriel* (call sign MAOS) in Liverpool on 29 September 1953 just five days after signing off the *Linguist* (call sign GQBC). Surprisingly, she didn't sail for some weeks. I became friendly with one of the cadets who invited me to stay with him in his home near East Grinstead in Surrey. They had a wide circle of friends. They had just opened a country house restaurant with a chef head-hunted from the Connaught Rooms. The social life was great. I met the comedian Jimmy Edwards several times in the local pub/club. The local charity was to support the rehabilitation of badly burned pilots, patched back to some appalling resemblance of humans by Dr Archie McIndoo, later Sir Archie, who was then the leading plastic surgeon in the country. In 1953 it was pretty basic. I met several of the surgeons who had become quite neurotic from the stress of what they were dealing with and the monsters they were producing. McIndoo's work made him world famous. Some of the victims made a brave effort to accept and live with the trauma and stress of their horrible faces. They formed the Guinea Pig Club in 1941, an exclusive drinking club which met annually until a final meeting in 2007 with just seventeen old veterans.

I returned to the *St. Merriel* and prepared for the long voyage to Buenos Aires on the River Plate. It was interesting for me, a young impressionable beginner, to be imposed into a close-knit band of mariners all from different backgrounds and marine training which had influenced their societal behaviour. I noted their different social aspirations and, in some cases, assumptions.

The officers of the coaster carrying coal from South Wales and Newcastle-upon-Tyne were local men mainly raised in the coalmining areas, and very down to earth.

The gentlemen on the oil tanker were reputed to suffer from 'tankeritis', a condition brought on by spending so much time aboard their tankers at sea that they had become remote from urban life.

The Liverpudlians aboard the Harrison ships sailed on relatively short return voyages to the West Indies where they island-hopped, socialising with the locals and enjoying their trips. They were typical Scousers – little side and a great sense of humour.

The officers aboard the South American Saint Line were rather more socially aspirational. Operating a cadet scheme where fees were paid by parents, some had studied in residential training colleges such as HMS *Conway* in the Menai Straits, HMS *Mercury* at the Hamble, HMS *Worcester* on the Thames and the *Arethusa* at Greenhithe. In 1953, such officers were proud of their alma mater.

What they all thought of a young, immature radio officer intruding into the group is unknown, but it was a little challenging for both parties. In the case of the *Merriel* matters got rather more complicated, as two of the officers were overtly erotic. The captain could not look anyone in the eye, not even a young RO. He looked over the shoulder of anyone he spoke to. He locked and bolted his cabin door at night, ate in his room, and as the voyage wore on became ever more reclusive. We tended to ignore him.

The first mate seemed OK at first. From some public school, a charming man with just a hint of insincerity in the charm, otherwise all right. He had an odd habit: when we reached Las Palmas, he disappeared without any warning. No doubt this was usual, and possibly expected. When he came back aboard after thirty-six hours, just before we sailed, unshaven and totally hung over, he slipped into his cabin for twelve hours. When he reappeared, nothing was said and all seemed normal. Given that he was one of three navigating officers responsible for navigating the ship on a twenty-four-hour basis this behaviour was very odd.

The second mate was fine and quite normal. As we sailed down off Finisterre, he came into the radio office to ask for help in getting the 'Pool' results. He got quite excited when he heard that he had three 'draws'. He threw a party that night to celebrate.

Next day, when I got the BBC on short wave, it transpired that forty thousand others had got three 'draws' and his winnings were just about £20. He was good-natured about it all and took it well.

The third mate was just a little older than me, about twenty-two, and unmarried. We were pals for the voyage.

One of the dangers in a flat calm ocean with a beautiful idyllic day is that it is easy to stand out on deck for an hour chatting. You easily forget that you have travelled twelve miles. We were in the Bay of Biscay enjoying such a chat one lovely morning, when the helmsman called out, 'look here, sir.' The entire ocean in front of us was covered with a huge fleet of Spanish fishing trawlers and we were heading into the middle of them. Short of stopping the ship, the mate took the wheel and gently steered our way through them as they scuttled out of our way. We held our breath that the captain wouldn't appear. He did come up shortly afterwards and fortunately didn't look back at our zig zag wake through the fishing fleet. We wondered later if he had noticed it but didn't have the guts to raise the issue. We sailed on.

The next morning at about 7.00 a.m. local time I was having breakfast with the first officer. There were two engineering officers at the next table. Not a ripple on the sea, no swell to remind you that you were at sea, making twelve knots, heading south by south west, everything right with the world.

Suddenly, without any warning the ship heeled over to an alarming angle. Everything went flying: breakfasts in laps, coffee pots in the air, and chairs falling over. Because of the good weather, nothing was tied down. The angle of the deck got worse and it was difficult to stand. Were we sinking? Had we hit something? Pulling ourselves up the stairs to the bridge we heard some heated voices. We quickly saw that we had done a U-turn and were now heading north back towards the UK. You can U-turn a car, possibly even a speedboat, but not an eight thousand-ton ship. Why? There wasn't a ship in sight.

The captain had the helm when we arrived and quickly handed it back to the helmsman. 'Back to 198, then, Helm,' he grunted, and slunk off the bridge.

Apparently, he had walked up to the bridge for his morning check with the Watch; he looked forward on this beautiful morning and saw the peak of Mount Teide, in Tenerife, straight in front. Mount Teide is twelve thousand feet high and can be seen for many miles. Forgetting that we were twenty miles away, he saw it as an immediate hazard, panicked, shouted to the helmsman, 'hard about.' The helmsman didn't understand the order so the captain pushed him out of the way, overrode the automatic pilot, and executed the turn himself. Stranger than fiction, quite mad and even dangerous, but there was more to come.

One night the mate and some of the engineers got quite drunk and decided to cause a scene with the captain. They banged on his cabin door for some time. When there was no response, they let off a foam-fill fire extinguisher under his door. No reaction, not a sound from the captain.

One of the jobs for deck officers every morning was to pump up water from the bottom tanks to the service tanks on the top deck, from which it was gravity fed down to the living accommodation. Water is a very precious commodity aboard ship, and wastage is abhorred. At lunch one day, the first officer had commented on the amount of water he had to replenish daily. It had hugely increased over the last ten days. He had asked the engineers to look for a possible leaking pipe, but nothing was found

On a very hot afternoon a few days later, I was on the bridge talking quietly with the officer of the watch, the second mate. This time of day is siesta time, when the officers off watch would sleep for some hours to allow for four hours duty during the night. The ocean was a sullen, motionless mirror, hardly a sound anywhere and yet! there was a sound of water exiting from one of the waste pipes. Nothing unusual in that, except that this stream was continuous. Had we found the leaking pipe? From the bridge we could identify that the outlet pipe was the waste pipe from the captain's bathroom. The captain was running his taps to waste. Why?

An urgent meeting was held, and we remembered that the captain had expressed his concern that the entrance to the River Plate had a sand bar at a depth of 29½ feet and we were drawing 29¾ feet. He would insist on timing our entrance to the top of the tide. But he was still worried that we might damage the ship. We found it hard to credit that he was breaking the prime rule about conserving water. And did he really believe that a few hundred gallons would alter the ship's draft? About 220 gallons of water weighs a ton and our ship weighed nearly 8,000. A few hundred gallons lighter would clearly make no difference. He had also forgotten that a sand bar is composed of sand – we could easily slide slowly over it. It was not a problem, but he was deliberately wasting our precious water reserves.

What to do? The team came up with a good plan. Playing to the captain's sick mind, a make-believe scene was set up, and I was there to enjoy it.

Imagine the captain entering the Chart Room to find a group of his officers studying the ship's loading diagram – a large blueprint showing a cross section of the vessel. The officers were worried; could the captain help them? The problem was that the ship had a draft of 29¾ feet when evenly loaded. Due to the leaking pipe (which could not be located) the water tanks at the rear of the ship were becoming depleted, losing their weight. This would upset the even balance of the ship and cause the front of the vessel to tilt downwards, to perhaps thirty feet or more.

Of course, the captain fell for the ruse – the mysterious loss of water ceased that day. This event was so evident of neuroses and simple stupidity that I marvel to this day how that man could retain a captain's position. Still, it made for an interesting voyage.

We spent some weeks in the Plate area between Buenos A and Rosario in Argentina and Montevideo in Uruguay – a wonderful experience.

Buenos Aries was my second experience in a major Hispanic city after Havana, but was far superior, and it opened my eyes to a new world. Coming from Ireland where only men frequented pubs which were truly spit and sawdust, it was a culture shock to meet a society which catered for all the family, '*Especialidad por Familias*'. Evening life ran from 8.00 or 9.00 a.m. to 1.00 or 2.00 a.m.. Streets were crammed with parents walking their children, often aged three or four. The city streets at 10.00 p.m. were like Grafton Street in Dublin on a Saturday morning, but lit with the bright neon lights of advertisements and restaurant names. Think of Barcelona and New York combined, and you'll be able to picture Buenos Aires. Huge, straight *avenidas* leading into historic *plazas*, one bigger than the next. My favourite was the Plaza Britannica, a huge concourse like Trafalgar Square. My favourite supper was beef steak, '*con dos huevos y patatas frittas con vasa de leche.*' Yes, I preferred milk to wine in those days.

Some of the ship's officers had previously met the English daughters of some expatriate management. They had travelled to school in the UK aboard the Saint Line ships. We were invited to some Christmas parties. The main event was an invitation to the New Year Dinner and Ball in the Hurlingham Club, with a champagne breakfast the following morning. The problem was how to dress; it was a black-tie affair but we had no dress uniforms.

Our Chinese stewards wore full white uniforms which we requisitioned, and when we put on our brass buttons, our epaulettes, and arm stripes, we were a pretty sight. We were pleased that some of our hosts assumed that we were the officers of RMS *Alcantara*, the Royal Mail high speed, 26,000 ton luxury liner. English Naval uniforms were a novelty at an expatriate 'do', where the crowd were probably bored with meeting the same people at every function. I remember chatting with the general manager of Ford Argentina. For some reason, he explained to me about the effect the high humidity had on the expatriates' marital sex life; aged twenty-one, did I really need to know this?

After this event, we now had to return the honours, so we rigged up the sun sheets on the boat deck, and found some coloured lights from somewhere – probably emergency lights from the lifeboats. I set up the music system and the Chinese chef plus stewards put up a really polished performance. It was a great success for a little cargo ship.

A week later, we were moored alongside a marsh area upriver from Rosario. The incessant noise of the huge bullfrogs plus the unpleasant humidity kept us awake at night, and we were not well disposed towards the bullfrogs. We all had too much to drink and it seemed a good idea to organise a bullfrog hunt; better still, have a competition. Thankfully, someone had the good sense to remember the mosquitoes. We kitted up with long trousers tucked into three layers of socks, hats, scarves and long sleeves. We split up into teams of two, one with a torch and one with a large bag, then into the swamps. With hindsight it was crazy and we could have lost a life, but happily it went well and we had the best of fun.

The frogs were the size of cats weighing about three kilos. They reacted well to our frog noises and were mesmerised with the torchlight so that it was easy to catch them and very satisfying. We could fit only three into a bag and returned to the ship after an hour or so.

The ship had one large communal shower room so we stopped up the plugs, turned on all cold taps and showers flooding the floor to a depth of about four inches. We then upended our bags and counted the catch. The frogs liked the cold water and we all had a great time while we refreshed ourselves with more beer or gin.

The next bright idea was to organise a frog derby to race them back along the pier to the shore line. Some frogs were up for it, but some went the wrong way, while others simply jumped off the pier side into the river.

The midsummer night was ending as the sky lightened; time for bed.

My last adventure in South America was a two-day trip to Montevideo, the capital of Uruguay. The city centre faces on to the sea with a long promenade where we berthed – almost at the end of the main street. The locals like to walk along the prom, so it is great for people watching. It is also a short walk into the city and the weather was pleasant.

Montevideo was a city created by the British and it had a slightly English atmosphere. There was an English hospital with English nurses who invited us to a dance there. A nice place, and one I would like to revisit.

The thing to buy there was Monte boots: calf length, good leather, lined with wool. I bought a pair for ten shillings (50p) and sold them some months later in Monaghan for £4.

As we left Montevideo we were fully loaded for the homeward journey, non-stop except for the usual top-up of bananas or tomatoes in the Canaries.

I was busy sending radio messages to the Wireless College in Manchester, organising a three-month study course for my Senior Telecommunication and Radio Certificates. I was not to know that this was to be my last voyage, the end of my time at the most pleasant finishing school you could imagine.

CHAPTER 5
MY CAREER IN ENGLAND

AFTER TWO YEARS AT sea I had decided to upgrade my qual-
ifications and went back to wireless college in February '54.
I finished a three-month course and obtained my First Class
Radio Officer Certificate in Radio and Electronics.

However, a difficult situation had arisen at home in Monaghan
and I was required to manage the situation. There had been
a fire in our shop which had disrupted our business but fortunately caused limited damage. My brother Brian, who had
been managing the shop, was unable to continue. I was required
immediately to help my mother.

When I arrived in Monaghan and assessed the situation, I found
that the damage could be quickly mended. Importantly, the cash
flow of the business had to be restored. I had the fire damage
repaired although it was difficult to lose the smell of smoke.

As soon as possible I organised a sale – the first ever in our
shop – and liquidated much of the (mostly old) stock . I agreed
an arrangement with our largest debtors, the Ulster Bank and
Eason's, to pay off old debts over six months.

I regarded Eason's as a critical supplier which we would need
to maintain the supply of newspapers and, importantly, books.
I met with the Sales Director and undertook to trade out our
debt within eight weeks.

I wasn't long back at the shop when I had a stroke of luck. The Irish distributor of Marvel comics on his first visit to Monaghan called to us first. I got quite excited by these attractive comics with Superman, Batman, and the rest and bought the entire stock from his van, paying him on the spot. My object was to gain an exclusive supply. The word spread quickly around our small town and the comics flew out the door. I rang the distributor and placed a standing order for several hundred every month, on condition he gave me exclusivity – which he did.

At that time, I was very much into reading good novels as soon as these were published and we soon got a reputation as the premier bookseller. I used to visit Eason's in Dublin every Thursday and could supply on Friday any books ordered up to Wednesday. We filled one of our windows with the latest bestsellers. I couldn't have done so well without the support of Eason's, who supplied advice, promotional material and credit to pay off our debt to them.

I also specialised in pens: Conway Stewart, Platignum and Parker. A few advertisements and special offers got us better sales and better margins. I also got support from Kapp and Peterson to help me offer an attractively-priced quality range of smoking pipes.

Our shop was located at the top of Dublin Street, so salespeople driving into town were likely to call first on us. This had happened with Marvel and others, so one evening, when a tired sales agent called in with a range of innovative chocolate clusters unlike anything on the market, I saw another opportunity. I bought his entire stock, paid him cash and asked him to call me in a month. We gave a small sample of these to the families buying the Marvel comics, and soon found that both were selling fast. We repeated the process, and again got exclusivity.

Within six months, we paid off our debts and I was quite enjoying the business. However, my mother's heart was not in it and I was ambitious for opportunities in a larger economy. My mother would move to Manchester where her sister Rose and husband Fred lived, so the decision was made to sell. We sold the business in January 1955 to a Mr Hackett, who bought it for his son, Patrick, whom I had known in St Macartans. We got £4,000 sterling.

We then held an auction and sold nearly everything. We travelled light, but I have always regretted selling the many fine antiques which my father had collected.

Still, a brave new world beckoned. Mum stayed with Aunt Rose and Uncle Fred until she bought a fine, four-bedroom semi-detached house: 64 Park Road, Stretford, about five minutes' walk from Aunt Rose. It was to be our home until 1963.

With my qualifications, I found it easy to get a job, and within a month was hired by Rediffusion as a service engineer. Rediffusion had established a business where they cabled up an entire district and provided a high quality sound service, from four broadcasting stations, delivered by cable – no interference. They also provided a sound reproduction system to large concerns such as the Kellogg's factory, the Manchester Royal Infirmary, Queens Hotel etc.

My job was to carry out routine and emergency maintenance on the company's installations. This required me to be on call on some weekends and holidays, including Christmas Day. I also worked as part of a four-man team installing new amplification stations. My boss was George Tickle and we became friends. I was best man at his wedding later that year.

My means of transport was a 50cc BSA Bantam motorbike, which I loved. It enabled me to learn my way around Manchester and how to handle traffic – a useful lead into driving.

I spent holidays with my sister Carmel, and Frank Egan. Carmel was very much my big sister. I loved her and she was always there for me along with her husband Frank who became my friend. She gave me driving lessons during my holidays and with the experience of her lessons I drove a Rediffusion van from Salford to Buxton and back. It was pretty hairy, with a few stalls and a lot of luck.

One stormy night, I skidded my motorbike on wet cobblestones in Salford, knocked myself out and finished up almost under a bus. My feelings weren't helped by my boss's concern expressed about the condition of the bike rather than me. I started looking for another job that week, something with a white collar and a car.

Within two months, in November 1955 I was hired by R.C.A. (The Radio Corporation of America) in a job which was white collar and provided a new car. I travelled down to London and collected a brand new Standard 8 from the main agents in Berkeley Square – very posh! The job offered little in the way of challenge or career prospects, but it was well paid and comfortable and at twenty-two I was entitled to enjoy myself.

My next-door neighbour, Alan Heap, had a hobby, building and racing stock cars at the Bellevue Race Track, and I helped him when I could. He had three young daughters and he was glad to have a young man around sometimes. I was always asking for a race and eventually he gave me two outings, racing stock cars at the Bellevue track. I enjoyed the excitement and the experience. An incredible sport – very rough and ready, but not dangerous.

Another friend, Ron Sillitoe, was an engineer in the nearby Trafford Industrial Park. Ron was older than me but shared my interest in Grand Prix racing which was just then enjoying an exciting period. Ron drove a 350cc Triumph monster and together we often visited Silverstone and Oulton Park to watch the big races. I continued this interest for some years, but 1955 was a seminal year, the year Stirling Moss, a home-grown hero, became a world figure. In May he won the Mille

Miglia, a really hairy road race over nearly 1000 miles around Italy through towns and villages with very little marshalling or safety barriers. Moss was the first Englishman to win, beating world champion Juan Fangio with an average speed of 95mph over more than ten hours. I have seen a Shell film of the race several times. In July, I was at Silverstone to see Moss in a British car, the Coventry Climax, beat Fangio in a Mercedes to win the British Grand Prix.

In the summer of 1956 I holidayed in Ireland. My friend Gerry Charlton, a newly qualified solicitor, had got his first job with a Dublin criminal lawyer who was defending Paul Singer. As I had a car and Gerry didn't, I chauffeured him with many legal tomes for him to discuss points of law with his client. Dr Singer had come into Ireland and bought Shanahan's Stamp Auctions which he used as a vehicle to allegedly swindle many with 'get rich quick' ideas about buying stamps from him at inflated prices. Only Singer got rich, but he was arrested and charged with an offence and incarcerated in Mountjoy Gaol. In rejecting the charge, he defended himself and required Gerry to bring him a constant supply of law books. The case was a 'cause célèbre' and ran for months. I seem to remember that Singer was acquitted on a technicality and left the country.

While working for RCA I had a lovely time with my new car and an easy stress-free job. I was a cinema sound engineer responsible for installing and maintaining high fidelity sound reproduction and amplification systems in cinemas throughout the North East, North West and North Midlands. I was required to visit towns and cities from Hull to Holyhead, from Crewe to Lancaster, staying in comfortable hotels and seeing hundreds of movies. These were the days before Elvis and Bill Hailey, but we had James Dean, Brigitte Bardot and films by Ingmar Bergman.

Despite the good time I was having, as spring '57 came in I felt that I had exhausted the potential of the job and I started to look around. My timing was fortunate. ShellMex and BP Ltd. were starting up a major initiative to introduce the new concept of oil-fired central heating to the cold, damp houses of Great Britain and Ireland. They were recruiting over a hundred staff.

Previously, the distribution of hot water in heating pipes and radiators had depended on the natural circulation by gravity of hot water and needed very large pipes to reduce friction. Such large pipes were suitable for use only in mansions and large buildings. When the National Coal Board proposed the concept of pumping hot water through small-bore pipes, Shell saw it as an opportunity to open up a huge new outlet for oil. Their foresight was truly innovative and was to raise the standard of living for millions. It would require extraordinary developments to create an entirely new industry; manufacturers must be persuaded of the opportunity to design and manufacture small domestic boilers, attractive slimline radiators and pumps. Wholesalers must be trained to stock and promote the systems. Suitable fitters and plumbers would be identified, enthused and trained in the new systems. They would be taught how to calculate heat requirements and install efficient low-cost heating. Turning bright young plumbers into heating engineers was the challenge. This was an ambitious programme, required a new Sales Division, and they were hiring. Age requirement was from twenty-four and I applied, stating my date of birth without highlighting that I was only twenty-three.

Interviews depend on the chemistry between participants, and my meeting with the Manchester branch manager was pleasant and successful. I was directed to London to meet the august Mr Chippendale, the father of fuel oil combustion in Britain.

Shell MEX House is not the tallest building in London, but it is arguably one of the most impressive. Located on the Strand overlooking the Thames, the sheer bulk reflects the power of its owners. Walking through the vast doors that morning, nervous before my interview, I had no idea that I was on the threshold of a career that would fulfil my every ambition for half a lifetime, a career that would eventually lead to this book.

Mr Chippendale was interviewing me for an appointment as an Industrial Fuel Supervisor. Known simply as Chip, he was a gentle, relaxed fatherly figure who first handed me a copy of his book *The Combustion of Oil* and brought me over to one of the two windows that decorated his large office. The view of the Thames far below was lovely. Later, with a cup of coffee in my hand and his patient support in a friendly informative conversation, I was able to recall my school-days knowledge of hydrocarbon combustion and, with his encouragement, to supplement it so that I could discuss it easily. When he approved me for further interviews for the Midland Division, in Birmingham, his imprimatur eased me through these subsequent events and I was soon into the company induction programme.

My introduction into Shell Mex and BP could not really be described as training; it was simply an osmotic process into many facets of the industry during a six-month probationary period, where one was observed to see if you were a 'good chap.' It was quite exciting and very enjoyable. To survive this period, one had to carry oneself comfortably with a wide cross section of English middle-class professionals, many older than my twenty-three years. I was grateful for my years in the Merchant Navy 'finishing school' which had knocked off many of my rough edges and helped me build my self-confidence.

A company the size of Shell Mex and BP had a constant intake of new recruits for divisions other than the central heating division. A sample would include real estate negotiators, architects, engineers, specialists in PR, HR, statistics, economics, marketing, and sales; every facet of a huge business. We all met on courses in Shell country clubs, on seminars, and on the job. I was sent to the Stanlow oil refinery for a week; to a shale mine near Grangemouth; on a delivery tanker for a week in Birmingham; with a retail rep for a week in Stratford; with an agricultural rep for a week in Shropshire; to a manufacturer of oil-burning equipment and to the Shell continuous combustion laboratories in Fulham for a week.

The premier Shell country club was the Node in Codicote, Herts. I spent three or four sessions there over my first years in the company, usually a week or two at a time. It had everything: squash, golf, snooker, a library, a bar and en-suite accommodation. The atmosphere of leather, polished brass, mahogany and burgundy carpets, made it the quintessential gentleman's club. We often wondered if we were being reported on, and I subsequently learned that we were.

Between all the various elements of my training I met a number of the new entrants on several occasions, including some from Ireland. People I remember were Eric Evans, an ex-captain of the English rugby team; Peter Yarrington, ex-captain of the RAF rugby team and subsequently General Secretary of the RFU; George Hespe, one of my domestic heating colleagues, had been a Fleet Air Arm pilot, as well as a C of E vicar who wanted a change. From Ireland, I met Pat Creagh, with whom I subsequently worked in Sligo; also Noel Harris – a brother of actor Richard (he was full of stories about him) and Ted Piggott, an Englishman working for Irish Shell as Domestic Heating Manager in Dublin. I would later report to him.

A memorable training course located me in a splendid hotel, the Royal Worcestershire Spa in Droitwich, a little-known small spa situated half way between Worcester and Birmingham.

We had a party there every night with the English cricket team who were also staying in the hotel as they played a test match at Edgbaston cricket ground. Peter May was the captain and strictly told his players to go to bed at 10.00 p.m. But as soon as he turned off his bedroom light, back down they came. I remember seeing Freddie Truman duck down behind the bar when Captain May made a check-up visit. He got away with it every night – a wild one.

After about eight weeks living in hotels, I was appointed to the Worcester branch and signed into an hotel on the banks of the Severn. Allowed two weeks to find accommodation, I soon found my way to a private house who took two full-time guests. The Bonhams were one of the most unforgettable families I've ever known. Mr Roger Bonham was Assistant Headmaster at the Royal Worcester College for the Blind. He taught maths and was World Champion of the blind chess players. He carried on games by post with Russian grand masters. He also liked to back horses, so mornings were exciting as the post arrived to announce a new move by a Russian chess master or a winner at yesterday's races. Roger made no allowance for his blindness and would blunder impatiently around the house crashing into chairs, a great character. His wife and their three children were like family to me. I was very happy there.

My work in setting up a domestic central heating service proceeded well and I enjoyed the fellowship of my Shell colleagues. Friday was a day to have several pints with them in the Royal Spa in Droitwich with a full lunch followed by treacle tart or sticky pudding. The afternoon was spent in the spa resting – what an introduction to business in England. A particular challenge was market day with the Branch Agricultural Rep, when we spent ten hours at the bar in the Feathers in Ludlow buying half pints while the farmers paid their bills in £20 notes.

Life is full of change and after about eight months I was told that I was to transfer out of Shell Mex and BP and to join Power Petroleum Co. with offices at 1 New Street, Birmingham. Power was a subsidiary of Shell Mex and had no industrial fuels division. Someone had decided to have it enter the fuel oil market as a second runner in the increasingly competitive market. The division had two Industrial Lubricant reps and I was the sole Industrial Fuel supervisor. The plan was that the other reps would feed me prospects and I would 'convert' them. At that time, most of British industry was still burning coal although the 'Clean Air Act' had become law in 1956. Industry had been given time to convert to a fuel combustion system which would reduce the emission of smoke. This created a great opportunity for the oil industry and began the slow decay of the British coal mining industry.

I was picked because I was the only single person in the division who could relocate easily. The fact that I knew nothing about heavy fuel oil or industrial applications was apparently irrelevant.

My transfer to a new job without any training was pretty typical of the Shell group, they did it several times. I hadn't even seen a steam boiler when I got the job, yet all the Power staff thought I was an expert industrial combustion engineer. I was now advising on the conversion of metal melting furnaces, baker's ovens and brick kilns. We even had a go at converting Dudley Crematorium from gas to oil. My strongest sources of knowledge were the sales reps of the boiler, burner and furnace companies who worked with us to develop prospects and convert them to oil. I learned on my feet, listened, studied, asked questions and looked wise. I found it all very interesting and in fact became fairly expert in the subject.

Social life was great. I rented a flat in City Road, Edgbaston, just off the Hagley Road, sharing with a Swiss and an Irish man. My friends Brian and Jimmy in Power took me under their wing. I liked singing, so they enrolled me in the chorus of the Crossed Keys Musical Society. I sang in *Lilac Time*, *Oklahoma*, *1066 and All That*, plus numerous company gigs. Brian also

signed me up for Round Table No. 50, City of Birmingham.
Together with Brian and Jimmy I started playing golf on Friday
afternoons and Saturday mornings. The Pro fee was half a
crown (two shillings and six pence, now 12½ pence). I never
became much good at golf. I also spent a lot of money driving Formula 3 racing cars at an embryonic racetrack in Castle
Comer in Wiltshire.

My Cricket Days – as bad as my golf

Meanwhile I holidayed regularly in Ireland and became
friendly with my colleagues in Irish Shell, Ted Piggott, now
in charge of the Irish domestic heating market, and my industrial fuel colleagues, Frank McArdle and Johnny Buggle. After
two years in Power Petroleum I now wanted to get back to
Ireland, so I put the word around in Dublin, especially with
Bill Murdoch, the Personnel Manager.

The following January I was invited to Shell Mex House on The Strand in London to meet the Irish Shell Sales Manager Jack Murphy. We had a pleasant chat and I was offered a job in Ireland: 'Take a month to wrap up your work in Power Petroleum and come to Ireland in March 1959.' I thought I was transferring to Dublin – I was in for a surprise.

CHAPTER 6
RETURN TO IRELAND

IT WAS A COLD Friday morning in April 1960 when I received the call from my friend Kevin.

'You are needed by the police to do an underwater search for a car thought to have gone over the highest cliff in Mullaghmore.'

When we arrived at the site, the police were there in force together with about fifty onlookers. The surf was monstrously high with a fourteen-foot swell breaking on the headland but there was a small natural harbour partially protected. It looked dangerous but it was up to me to try. The story was that a Ballyshannon man was missing and there seemed to be evidence that a car had gone over the top of the cliff. No one was sure, and the police wanted me to find out if there was a car under the water and if there was a body in it…

As I look back to my arrival into Dublin in 1959, I realise how things had changed since my departure. I was travelling in comfort on a drive-on ferry rather than on a cattle boat but more relevantly, I had changed. After eight eventful years of study, the Merchant Navy, and business, I was more mature and better able to manage and grow my career.

Arriving by the B & I mail boat at the North Wall in Dublin on a sunny March morning in 1959 was a most pleasant experience. My friend – and now my boss – Frank McArdle, Fuel Oil Manager, met me and brought me to a hotel. Later that day I met, Bert Crossland from Manchester, Industrial Lubricants Manager, and Ted Piggott, my old friend from early days in Shell Mex, now Domestic Heating Manager. A friendly and supportive bunch.

Later on that day I enquired where I would be picking up my car and was told that a Hillman Hunter was ready for me at the railway station. Which railway station? There is only one station in Sligo. Why Sligo? That's where you are going – didn't anyone tell you?! I'm a combustion engineer with serious industrial experience in the British Midlands – why Sligo? This was typical of Shell. Mysterious decisions and poor communications.

The word was that the Shell gang in Sligo were a hard-drinking bunch and I was advised to stay away from the Grand Hotel. The branch area covered all points north and west of Drogheda, Roscrea and Galway. There were four general sales reps and a distributor, the Donegal Oil Company, which had two excellent sales personnel.

With my wide experience in different sectors, I was to be the technical sales supervisor on 1) domestic oil-fired central heating 2) the industrial fuel market and 3) the lubricants market. As such, I reported to three divisional managers, Frank, Ted, and Bert, as well as my branch manager, Niall O'Connell.

It was a good time to return to Ireland. With de Valera and most of the old guard gone, Seán Lemass was proving to be a strong leader. Dr Ken Whitaker had just introduced his First Programme for Economic Expansion and a new industrial development programme had begun, giving me lots of opportunities. I was the only industrial fuel oil specialist in the west and, with a strong network of support, I was very successful. To the best of my knowledge, we won the fuel, oil and lubricants business in every new factory during my time there.

Irish Shell was starting up a major initiative to introduce the new concept of oil-fired central heating to be marketed to the cool, damp houses of Ireland. It was proposed to have many properties heated by small bore pipes fitted with pumps to circulate hot water from purpose designed oil-fired boilers. Shell saw it as an opportunity to open up a huge new market for oil. Their foresight was incredible and would raise the standard of living for millions.

This was an extraordinary opportunity, to create an entirely new industry. Designers and manufacturers must be persuaded of the real opportunity to produce new small boilers, attractive slim line radiators and pumps. Suitable fitters and plumbers would need to be identified, enthused and trained in the new systems. They would be taught how to calculate heating requirements and design efficient, effective and low-cost systems. Turning bright young plumbers into heating engineers was the challenge and I was one of three men to introduce it to Ireland.

It was helpful that Irish Shell was the leader in this market, and I had the freedom to use my emerging entrepreneurial skills. I picked the best plumbers and trained them, picked the best hardware stores like Meldrum's in Sligo, McDonalds in Galway. I installed working showpiece boilers, teaching their staff how to market domestic central heating and which plumbers they should use. I certificated suitable approved merchants and Shell-approved installers. I also had to teach myself and absorb a great deal of new information. I learned how to calculate the heat requirement for different situations and locations. I learned how to design heating systems and calculate pipe sizes and border sizes. I was soon designing central heating layout for hotels, churches, shops and small factories.

Oil fired central heating (OFCH) was so new that in 1959 our iconic housewife of the future was branded 'Mrs 1970'. June Ganley was an attractive young woman, and she visited Ireland frequently. Shell's advertising agency, McConnell's, had invented the story that I and two colleagues were the three Knights of the Warm Home and displayed our three life-sized cut out figures along with June Ganley in a chic window on Grafton Street in Dublin. At that time I was trying to attract a young lady, Helen Raftery, but wasn't making much progress, so I was encouraged when I heard she had brought her friends to see me there.

Author's note: It is strange to look back to 1960 and accept how successful that program was. Central heating is now an accepted requisite in most new houses.

<hr/>

Spring was breaking out in the west and I was having a pleasant social life. Sligo and Rosses Point are at their best in summertime and I soon met a group introducing water skiing, starting with one speedboat and some home-made skis. I was introduced to Brian Raftery, a lifelong friend, to Kevin Murray, a clever do-gooder, and lots of others. Enthusiastically we created the County Sligo Water Ski Club and trained hard at the three disciplines: slalom, trick skiing and jumping. Brian Raftery and I progressed to national level while Alan Murray won the European tricks medal at Trier, Germany. I won the Irish National Junior Slalom championship but didn't perform well at trick skiing and was very poor on the ski jump, rarely landing safely. I left my blood on every ski jump in the country and still have scars to show for it.

Loved slalom waterskiing

I also joined in dinghy sailing and crewed in GP14's sailing in Lough Gill until we moved to Rosses Point where we built a fine club house and launching ramp. The club is still thriving. When my brother-in-law, Brian Raftery, moved up to a Westerly yacht I crewed for him and had some great offshore sailing up the Donegal coast and down to Clare Island. Our few visits to that island were memorable. Brian would call on the yachting frequency asking for a lobster dinner. As we sailed into the bay, we saw Mrs O'Connor rowing out to the lobster pots. A creamy Guinness and fresh lobster was a nice finish to a day's sailing.

A memorable event was when nine of us hired three yachts in Majorca and sailed around the island. One evening, as we sailed across the Bay of Palma, our fleet under the command of Stuart Greer tried to make the Barcelona Ferry give way to sail. The ferry won.

There was little tennis available at that time but some years later Helen and I were founder members (and life members) of the Co Sligo Tennis Club. A local doctor, Paddy Quinn, donated part of his land to the infant club, a walled garden, perfectly sized for six hard courts. The club blossomed and became a great addition to Sligo's amenities. Helen, who played inter-county tennis as well as squash, donated a permanent cup for the girls Under 16's Singles Championship.

When I lived in Birmingham, my colleagues had encouraged me to join them on the municipal golf course, but I was not much good. Persuaded to keep it up, I took lessons in Rosses Point from Johnny McGonigle but continued to make no progress and after several years Johnny pointed out that I would never make a golfer. Finally, after yet another frustrating game, I gave it up for ever.

I was interested in flying and joined the new Aero club and started taking lessons; initially we were flying out of a large field near to Coloney but soon moved to a more suitable site in Strandhill. Money was required for start-up expenses and I donated £500. The Aero club continued and led to the development of the Sligo Regional Airport.

As a close friend of Brian Raftery, I was often a guest in the Raftery house for lunch on the occasional Sunday or holiday. I first met Helen on her Christmas holiday in December 1959, but we both had other interests, hers in Manchester and mine in Germany, so we remained friends at that time

When I learned that four serviced apartments were being developed, I was quickly into the race and got one on the top floor. These apartments were simply fabulous, and fully serviced for just £3 weekly. As the other three apartments were rented by friends of mine the joint parties were special and the 'Bachelor flats' soon became known as the place to be invited to. We four became lifelong friends.

For our water-ski clubhouse, we rented a large Victorian bungalow in an idyllic location on the Garavogue river. We added a large floating dock capable of mooring up to six speed boats in its small harbour, which soon became a water centre for friends and canoes as well as a serious training facility. It also gave us space to hold competitions and to run large barbecues. There were two bedrooms unused in the large property, and I rented these from the club as my home for a few months. It was a heavenly place where I could walk down the front lawn to the water's edge and feed the swans.

Living in Sligo was not only fulfilling, it was exciting and full of interest.

One of my friends was a truly outstanding man – Kevin Murray, socially conservative and with hands and a mind that could tackle anything. Very much a lateral thinker. We had many adventures. I was a keen scuba and snorkel diver; Kevin used my underwater skills and together we laid down the most accurate water ski slalom course, buoys anchored to the riverbed, measured to the millimetre and a system of tubes and boys which allowed for the rise and fall of the river. We also helped to build and grease a ski jump.

My daughter Sinead and myself in diving gear. Sinead is CEO of Yogandha.Com QV

An interesting experiment arose when the police offered Kevin a crashed Jaguar, a total write-off. Kevin took the engine for possible future use. He had a powerful ski-boat, a Moonfleet which had a two-litre Ford engine. In discussion with a marine engineer friend, we understood that the speed of a boat was based on the ratio between length and width almost irrespective of power.

We weren't quite sure, so Kevin decided to find out. He fitted the Jaguar engine and set out to time the race over a measured mile. The speed went up from 32 to 32.5 mph. The marine engineer was right but where had all the power gone? We had used gallons of petrol. I had one of my brainwaves and slipped over the side using a mask to examine the propeller. The large eight-inch blade had been worn down to stubs, how? Why? The answer suddenly hit me … cavitation. From my knowledge of pumping lubricating oil, I knew that when a pump – or in this case a propeller blade – rotates through a fluid, it generates cavities or bubbles on the low pressure side which collapse when they move into the pressure side of the pump or blade. This produces strong shock waves in the water that attack and damage the blades. I had long been aware of this phenomenon in theory but had never imagined how powerful it could be.

Kevin was always full of surprises but one Friday in April 1960, he surpassed himself. I had lunched in my apartment and was ready to go back to the office when he called me and said that I was needed. I protested that I was due at work and couldn't go, but he explained that I was needed by the police to do an underwater search for a car that was believed to have gone over the highest cliff at Mullaghmore. He impressed on me, 'It is not a matter of choice; it is something you're expected to do. I'll collect you in a few minutes.'

I collected my flippers, mask, and snorkel and we set off. Neoprene wet suits were very expensive at that time – perhaps two months' salary, and I couldn't afford one. I had my old red woollen sweater for heat and it kept me warm underwater for many adventures until I found a reasonably priced wet suit. But I wasn't looking forward to the cold Atlantic in April.

When we arrived at the site I was surprised at the level of public interest. The paparazzi were there and trying to photograph me, but the Gardaí kept them back. I was more interested in the sea conditions, which were frightening. The huge Atlantic swell was bursting onto the rocky shore in a frenzy of spume and whitewater. The conditions broke all the rules about scuba diving and under normal circumstances I would never have entered the water. There was a man missing, and a car missing and no one was sure exactly what had happened. The Gard wanted me to see if there was a car under the water and if there was a body in it. It was dangerous but it was up to me to try.

My concerns were the real chance of being backwashed out to the open sea; alternately, the large swell might hurl me on to the jagged rocks; and finally, whether there would be any visibility, as the cove was full of foaming white water. The police organised some rubber tyres at my point of entry to allow a safe exit and stretched a hefty rope across the mouth of the inlet with a number of men at each end so that I could cling on to it in the event that I was being pulled out to sea.

It turned out to be an easy job and was over quickly. There was no back wash and I could manage the swell easily. When I went down to about ten feet the white water cleared and I saw the car at about twenty feet. Both doors were open. There was no body, but the steering wheel was crushed forward as though by a body on impact.

When I reported this, I was asked to dive again and attach two ropes to the car. As I was using a snorkel and no air tank this took several dives, but I succeeded and the car was quickly pulled up onto the rocks. My main problem at this stage was the cold and as I exited the water the police wrapped me up in thick blankets and fed me hot tea and whiskey. By the time I was dressed, Kevin quickly urged me back into the car to avoid the paparazzi. Thanks to Kevin, I avoided being photographed, although the story was on the front page of the *Sunday Independent* and the *Sunday Press*. The *Sunday Express* had a typical amusing headline: 'Frogman Freddie dives again.' The *Independent* and *Press* described me as an employee of Irish Shell, and I got a lot of positive feedback from colleagues and even from the MD.

The year passed quickly and when Christmas came, Brian's sister Helen came home, and I got a chance to meet her again. When we threw a party in the Bachelor Flats she was, of course, invited. I was getting interested.

I had another underwater chore from Kevin Murray during that year. One of the Limerick Steamship Co cargo vessels had grounded on a previously unknown rock at the Deepwater quay. The rock had pushed the pintle up about six inches. The pintle is the huge bolt on which the rudder turns. The captain knew there was damage and would need to be dry-docked but he needed to know the extent of the damage. Was the pintle broken or cracked? Had it impacted onto the propeller? This knowledge would decide whether he needed a tug to tow him or whether he could sail independently. Depth was twelve feet; I had no underwater camera or photography skills and anyway the visibility was poor as we were right beside the sewage outlet from Sligo town. It was a most unpleasant dive and I was conscious of human waste floating past me. It took three dives before I got a clear picture in my mind which I was able to sketch once I had dried off. Damage was limited to a bent pintle and the propeller was not damaged. The ship sailed the following morning.

After a hot shower I went back to visit Brian and meet his sister Mary and Gerry Owens who had married earlier that year. Gerry was appalled that I would dive in such polluted water and he fed me whiskey to kill the bugs. He was shocked that I hadn't charged a hefty fee as I had saved the shipping company several thousand pounds. I explained that I was one of Kevin's do-gooders. He didn't approve, but the whiskey did the trick and I didn't get sick.

My friendship with my German girlfriend had faded and I was more than a little interested when I learned that Helen had decided to leave Manchester and move to the US to work in Michigan where her older brother Michael worked as a doctor. She would live in Sligo for six months while waiting for her work visa.

By this time, we had a large collection of mutual friends in Sligo who would go out together and it was natural that Helen and I would meet. Additionally, I had the advantage of being Brian's friend and visiting their home regularly gave me an advantage. It wasn't long before I asked Helen for a date. Her sights were on America, excited by a new adventure, but it would take six months for the work visa to arrive. I decided that I would try to meet her every day or, if out of town, to talk to her every day.

I can't remember how many times I asked her to marry me, I think it was eleven before one day she said yes. We both thought it was a great secret but I think it was probably expected.

Our wedding day was 30 August 1962; we were married in Sligo Cathedral by the Bishop of Elphin, Dr Hanley. Helen's sister, Joan, and her friend, Augusta, were bridesmaids. When we walked down the aisle and out into the open we were greeted by an archway of water-skis, a total surprise but a lovely one.

Wedding celebration with water skis arch

During our honeymoon in the Hotel Miramar in Hammamet, a luxurious Moorish palace, we met a friendly charming Englishman, Jeremy, taking a few days R&R after a harrowing trip to Rwanda Burundi where a brutal ethnic cleansing was taking place. The Hutu tribe who outnumbered the ruling Tutsis had risen against them and driven them out of the country (a shocking sequel to this occurred again in 1994, when the children of these Tutsis would return and precipitate one of the most bloody massacres in history, over a million murdered).

Jeremy proved to be excellent company and we had a good time together. When he left us he gave me his card privately. He was Jeremy Thorpe MP, a future leader of the Liberal party, who later became involved in a scandal resulting in his resignation.

Back in Sligo, Helen and I were happily settling down to an exciting and hopefully rewarding future. Our finances allowed Helen £5 pounds weekly for housekeeping, this to include her cigarettes and a daily *Irish Times*. We had no TV but enjoyed the radio and the big band music of the early 1960s. Helen's family were part owners of the cinema in Sligo, so we enjoyed free movies.

My water sporting activities continued. The sport of snorkel and scuba diving was in its early days and not that prevalent but the Gardaí knew of my diving skills. Whenever a diver was needed, I got the work – all pro bono, of course. An English doctor on a fishing holiday lost his outboard off the boat in Lough Eske in Donegal. He had not taken a bearing but thought he knew the spot! Without a bearing, an underwater search is bound to fail but I still spent a frustrating half hour diving in the cold black water, to find nothing. However, my efforts were appreciated and Helen got a present of a lovely make-up case from Weirs of Grafton Street.

A more productive dive, but a sad one, was searching for a body of a young man who had drowned in Rosses Point the previous day. There were five boats trawling for the body, but I was the only diver and quickly found it. It was a sunny day; Helen was sitting on the beach but would not have been able to see me lift the corpse into the boat.

Early in the New Year Helen realised that she was pregnant and in September 1963 our son Peter was born. His arrival turned us into a family, and we were such proud parents. Helen's housekeeping went up to £7.50 per week to feed our increased family.

In 1964 I received a proposal to partner in a water ski/scuba diving school in Tossa De Mar on the Costa Brava in Spain. The idea was that we would join another couple managing a combined water ski and dive school. As we both loved the sun and water sports, it was an attractive idea. Leaving our precious little boy Peter in the care of my big sister, we went to Spain. Helen taught water skiing while I taught scuba diving.

I had some unusual dives in the warm Mediterranean. In the bay of Estartit there are three spires of rock rising from a depth of about fifty metres. We swam up a natural underwater tunnel through the rock and found an iron ring fashioned into the rock at a depth of fifteen metres. How did it get there?

Local fishermen loaned the dive school their boats without charge so that we could provide offshore dives. We paid our way by early morning forays down to the seabed where we collected sea slugs for the fishermen's bait. A tame Grouper lived in a hole in the rocks and allowed me to stroke it, a unique experience.

We lived in a caravan on the beach and shared the experience beside a happy young group including a German girl, a Canarian and the two potential partners. After a long day in the sun we enjoyed our Cuba Libras, rum and coke, for which we paid 2.5cents. We found the mix too strong and were knocked out the first night. When a fresh bottle of rum was required, I offered to pay for it. 'Nonsense, there's lots in the store, just refill the bottle,' I was told. Under the caravan I found a large five-gallon carboy half full of rum. To fill the bottle, I used the same funnel that we used to pour petrol into the speedboat engines. The rum was in fact 100% illicit hooch. It didn't do

us any harm. This adventure was enjoyable but we decided not
to risk our limited capital on a speculative start-up business.

When we think of entrepreneurs, let's not forget Helen. After
all, she married me.

During our long life together, she has never hesitated to
join me in my adventures and none more so than in June 1963,
when the Dublin Garda Diving team contacted me via the Sligo
Guards inviting me on an adventure dive. It was proposed to
investigate a wreck which had sunk on a reef some miles north
of Inistrahull Light House itself some six miles north of Malin
Head. Helen came along for the fun, even though she was seven
months pregnant. Two of the Garda divers had brought their
wives and we met them at Malin Head harbour.

The interest in the wreck arose from an event in the 1950s
which has never been explained to this day. It concerned a ship
from the UK bound for China which was reported to have a
load of armaments, although that country was under an arms
embargo. This would be an explosive story if it became public.
Was it true? The ship hit a rock and broke in two. Half of the
ship sank quickly while the other half stayed afloat. The UK
press zeroed in, reporters trying to board the vessel while the
skipper used a shot gun to repel them before it sank.

Before the second half sank, the British army were allowed
by the Irish authorities to shield off part of Malin harbour
and bring the 'cargo' ashore in secrecy to be rapidly transited
to Northern Ireland. It had been a 'cause furore' at the time.
The Dublin divers were curious to investigate the first sunken
half which had not been unloaded. Boarding a twenty-five-
foot open fishing boat we set off onto the deep Atlantic swell,
which was about six metres; one minute, able to see the light

house and horizon, then only the grey walls of the swell insight. There was no white water, no sudden breaks in our rhythmic silent waltz in the swell.

Reaching the lighthouse, we were welcomed ashore and settled Helen and the other two ladies in the company of the keeper, who was glad to have visitors. They would of course be able to watch us as we set off for the dive site. I should explain that a powerful swell is relatively harmless until whipped up by the wind or, as in this case, by a jagged rock. When we got up on site, we found an angry maelstrom of boiling white water. No problem. Approached from fifty metres at five metres depth below the white water, visibility would be good. However, the dive leader reported that the steel plates of the wreck had burst their welded seams and were pointing up, very sharp and likely to seriously hurt a diver swept onto the hull by the swell. That dive was cancelled but we went back to the lee of the lighthouse where we enjoyed still clear water at eighteen metres and good fish life.

I brought home a basket of sea anemones.

Helen had grown up in a suburb of Sligo but had always wanted to live near the town centre. She asked me to find a home near the Post Office. I hunted for a suitable site and found a garden fronting on to Union Street, three hundred metres from the Post Office. I bought it from Miss Roulette for £170 and built two semi-detached, three-bedroomed houses. The total cost was £4000 for the two and I sold one for £4000, leaving us a new house free of cost: our first house. We moved into it in 1965.

At that time I heard some interesting stories of Helen's father starting up his company, the Western Wholesale Co. It needed the usual banking facilities but the only bank interested was the Ulster Bank and business was proceeding well. Then de Valera short-sightedly declared an economic war on England. 'Burn everything that's English except their coal,' was the mood of the day, so Joe Raftery couldn't be seen trading in the Ulster Bank, a Belfast and therefore British bank. What to do? After some smart thinking, it was agreed that the Munster and Leinster Bank would front the operation, handling lodgements, withdrawals, cheque clearances and the like, while the Ulster Bank would be the account holder. It worked well and the public never knew.

Another story concerned the Civil War. As the two forces needed victuals, units from both sides would occasionally pull into the WWC yard seeking provisions, and no mention of payment. When the conflict ended, the WWC sent the bill for both sides to the winners. They were paid in full.

During this period, my work in Irish Shell was going well, but I was beginning to feel stifled. My success in making some real money by building the Union Street houses had shown me that I could do it. Maybe it was time to get started.

CHAPTER 7

ENTRÉE TO ENTREPRENEURSHIP

WHEN I WAS GROWING up I had never heard of an entrepreneur – although now the word seems to be everywhere – so I had no idea why my mind was constantly spotting opportunities, raising ideas and asking questions, like why things were being done that way or was there a better way?

As a child I'd lie in bed and visualize my bedroom cupboard full of chocolate bars, ready to sell to my friends. I was planning my first business. From a very early age I wanted to be an independent operator. Even playing Cowboys and Indians I couldn't see why all the 'White Hats' advanced through the woods in a bunch. Aged seven, my strategy was to make a wide circle and ambush the opposition from the rear. The praise from the big boys was rewarding.

Growing up and helping in our shop was frustrating. I could see that it was dark and poorly-lit, with deep counters to keep the customers in their place. Neither of my parents knew anything about marketing or presentation, nor did I, but I could see that modern shops offered bright and inviting open access for the shoppers to see the goods. Eventually, I persuaded my mother to introduce fluorescent lighting which improved matters but we never developed the business and eventually sold it. Soon afterwards, it was bought by Wellworth's, who did exactly what I would have liked to have done if I had known and had the finance.

I kept on trying … When I worked for the Radio Corporation of America, RCA, they produced a beautiful High-Fidelity record player in an attractive cabinet specially for the US army camps in England. I was responsible for servicing their sound equipment in many cinemas and it occurred to me that cinemas had a captive footfall of patrons. Why not market the record players in the Atrium of the cinemas who are actually using RCA sound systems?

The manager of the Apollo Cinema in Lime Street, Liverpool, was enthusiastic and passed the suggestion up the line. I approached my manager in Manchester and when he showed no interest, I wrote to our London HQ who cynically passed it back to my manager. It never happened.

Many of these ideas were simply that: ideas with no strategies or business plans and were quite properly ignored or perhaps resented. I had to learn that an idea is cheap; it's turning it into a successful operation that is the challenge.

I had no idea how to start or fund a business and therefore made some silly mistakes. Working in Birmingham selling heavy fuel oil I noted the difference between our prices to the customer and the landed price of oil at the port. Off I went to the Russian Embassy in London, where I had an appointment to meet the Commercial Attaché. He received me graciously and quoted me a price per ton for an eight thousand-ton tanker. Yes, he would supply me, if I paid at point of departure from Russia. I then met the manager of Lloyd's main bank in New Street, Birmingham, and asked him for the money. Again, he was polite, but at some point I must have realized that it wasn't doable, because I never went any further with the idea. This was understandable as I had no money. I had a lot to learn. A rumour of my enquiries leaked back to Shell and was ignored. It was naïve and foolish.

In the spring of 1957, I was twenty-three, and my life was flying by with little to show for it. I was ambitious and very restive, ready for a challenge, and beginning to realize I wanted to manage something worthwhile, to do something creative. And I realized that my suggestion for selling record players through the Apollo cinema was ill-considered and foolish. It was another mistake. I would probably make many mistakes but that wouldn't stop me trying.

With hindsight, I can rationalize today that this ambition was the first definable birth pang of entrepreneurship. At this stage I had never even dreamed of running my own business let alone starting one up from scratch. I certainly didn't consider myself an entrepreneur and wanted only to get a management position that met my need for challenge and responsibility. Later in my career I set out to discover the reasons and motivation that prompted me into a series of start-up adventures, a practice repeated by a number of my children. I decided to find out more about entrepreneurs, how they differ from other businesspeople and how they are defined.

The word entrepreneur comes from the thirteenth century French verb 'entreprende' which means 'to undertake a task'. In the eighteenth century, a Kerryman from Ballyheigue, an economist, entrepreneur and sometime banker, Richard Cantillon, wrote his seminal *Essay on the Nature of Commerce in General* and was later accredited by Joseph Schumpeter as the originator of economic theory. One of his followers, Jean Batiste Say, also a businessman, probably added the 'eur' which change the verb into a noun, i.e. a person who undertakes a task. Over the decades there have been many studies to define the difference between a business manager and an entrepreneur, but it seems to me two are outstanding. In 1983, Professor Howard Stevenson, Harvard Business School, defined entrepreneurship as 'the pursuit of opportunity beyond reserves controlled'. The term was largely accepted but I prefer the more intuitive understanding by Professor Joe Schumpeter, also a Harvard Don, who finessed the situation better, I believe, with the title '*Unternehmergeist*'; that is, 'Enterprise with spirit'.

It was also at this point in 1957 that I discovered that the ShellMex and BP company was establishing a new marketing division and were seeking salespeople with a technical background. It seemed a suitable occupation for me and when I was hired, I was truly absorbed for many years in a wide range of duties which kept my interest and provided outlets for my creative drive.

However, by 1967, I had worked for Shell for ten years. I had met every challenge the market had thrown at me. I was on a good salary so it wasn't about money but I had ambitions beyond the comfortable niche I was occupying. Feeling frustrated, I raised my hand for the first time to enquire what my prospects were. Irish Shell's CEO, Barney Nolan, met me in his office – another first – and promised me that I would be promoted to a supervisory position in head office in Dublin in a few years.

I went home feeling encouraged and it was a few days before I realised that a small promotion meant little in the huge Shell machine. We would still be jumping to London's tune, which in turn would be jumping to the Royal Dutch Shell tune, a tiny cog in a large machine. I came to the conclusion that I didn't belong in corporate business. I wanted to be my own boss.

Meanwhile, social events were conspiring to help me find a way to attempt lift off.

One evening, a business associate called into our Union Street house and persuaded, indeed insisted, that I should join him and a group of other young men who were planning to start a Junior Chamber of Commerce in Sligo. Our group was positive and decided to proceed. The Senior Chamber of Commerce saw no need for a second chamber and the County Manager refused to meet us. We then contacted the National Jaycee office in Dublin and formed our chamber. A committee was formed and I was appointed Public Relations Officer.

In one of our first projects, the *Visitor's Guide to Sligo*, I was the production editor and quickly learned that I could out-match the performance of two of my team. They were both managers of factories; why was I just a sales rep? For years I had outperformed the competition, Esso and Caltex, but that was a corporate achievement. I had no previous experience of working in a small group in a real business situation, pitting my efforts against theirs. I was truly surprised to discover that my drive, energy and achievements surpassed my teammates.

This experience in Jaycee gave me the self confidence that I could make it on my own.

For the first time I faced the fact that I was probably a closet entrepreneur and that I needed my own dream, a project or a product that I could nurture into a business. I had a young family to look after so caution was necessary.

By this stage I had an idea and was formulating a plan to start my own business. When working in Birmingham I had noted that one of our customers was recycling waste sump oil from vehicle engines for sale as a fuel. Combustion of fuel oil was my speciality and I knew the industry in detail, placing me in a prime position to consider the proposition in terms of supply, costs, logistics, technology and market. I got busy researching the possibilities. From the statistics of motor oil sales in the Republic I calculated that about a million gallons of waste oil could be recovered together and another three hundred thousand gallons in Northern Ireland. I believed that only an all-Ireland business would be viable.

I worked out a system of planned collection which could support a service to the entire island. 'Don't call us, we'll call you,' meant that we could plan efficient truck-routing based on customer storage and output. The object was to arrange for a timely service and a worthwhile collection quantity. Assuming I could process the waste oil, the question was where to locate the plant, and importantly, who would buy the recycled oil? Unlike the industrial Midlands of England where there were many furnaces used by metal craftsmen and light industries, the opportunities in Ireland would be limited. The main fuel oil-users here were brick yards, grass drying, blood drying, fish meal drying, seaweed drying, cement works and large industrial boilers. I had to be careful in approaching potential customers in case Shell discovered my plans or in case I gave away the idea to a potential competitor.

My success in building the two houses in Sligo and my adventures in Spain had encouraged my entrepreneurial drive which was nearing explosion point. My capital was limited and if I couldn't find a suitable route to oil recycling, I had my eyes open for other possible opportunities. I was now committed to Harvard economist Schumpeter's *'Unternehmergeist'* (that is, 'Enterprise with Spirit'); I was on a mission. It had taken some for me to waken up. I was now following my dream and nothing or nobody would stop me.

At this time Charlie Haughey was Minister for Fisheries and Agriculture and was seeking to stimulate growth in these two areas. Large grants were available for new glasshouse construction and for the purchase of correctly-sized trawlers. As I had sufficient capital to invest in a fishing business I approached Bord Iascaigh Mhara as a possible investor, to have this option parallel my horticulture planning.

The main glasshouse development was in north county Dublin and Shell made me responsible for getting our share of this new market. The mushroom industry was expanding fast and I was also interested in this sector. Part of my involvement required me to get close to the movers and shakers in the industry, attending conferences in the Department's Glasshouse Research Centre in Kinsealy. I soon got to know the head man, Dr Michael Woods, and the head of the mushroom sector, Cathal McCann, along with many of the growers.

I found it impossible to secure guaranteed customers for my recycled oil which was understandable as I didn't have a product for anyone to test. I therefore made an important strategic decision which would influence the nature, shape and timing of my first major entrepreneurial adventure.

I decided to adopt a hen and egg approach.

I would establish and grow my own high energy-consuming business and introduce recycled oil as a fuel at a later stage. This would give me the opportunity to generate a cash flow which would be needed and to develop manufacturing procedures for an acceptable product.

There were few industrial furnaces available and the only high fuel opportunities that I could identify were in the mushroom and tomatoes industries. Mushroom culture requires a lot of steam for sterilization, and glasshouses need much heating. I set out to study the many aspects of such undertakings: capital, markets, location and growing technology. Location was important for collection of waste oil and for speed in getting the mushrooms to market. For much of 1966 I studied the technique of growing mushrooms together with operational details of composting, steam disinfection and marketing, I finally decided not to go into mushrooms and Cathal McCann asked me for my file and seemed pleased with the information I had assembled. Cathal was head of Kinsealy by this time.

During 1966 I was looking for small pockets of land near Dublin for the oil plant. I was also considering the development of a caravan park and in fact bid unsuccessfully on land in Balbriggan. I was considering the manufacture of holiday caravans or perhaps I could build up a business importing wigs from China.

As I was involved in developing Shell's interests in the expanding glasshouse industry, I was learning a little about the necessary environmental regime for glasshouse crops, tomatoes, cucumbers, peppers and lettuce. I was becoming friendly with the larger contractors supplying the heating equipment.

One of my erstwhile colleagues in Shell, Raymond O'Flynn, had not fitted well in the corporate market, had left Shell and taken control of Clyde Fuel Systems, a small Scottish company specialising in boilers. In early 1967 he asked me to join him as Industrial Sales Manager. Managing Director Raymond would focus on the domestic market. My job would be to import and sell steam boilers from an American boiler company, York-Shipley. This was a challenging proposal. Our second child, Suzanne, was due in March. How could I sell up and move my young family to Dublin, away from Helen's home town and all our friends, to live in a city where we knew few and to a job where I might not succeed? On the other hand, it was one step towards being my own boss. We had agreed that I would have autonomy in running my industrial department my way, which I did with great success,

Not many women due to deliver a baby would have the courage to support such a critical change of location and career, but Helen has always shown great courage and strength. Suzanne was born on 29 March in the middle of the night. Helen remembers that she couldn't take the smile off her face for weeks, she was so pleased that the new arrival was a baby girl. In those days, we had no way of knowing the gender of a baby before delivery.

By March I decided to make the break. I resigned from Shell, joined Clyde and in April, with a four-week-old baby and a three and a half-year-old son, we convoyed to Dublin, me pulling a trailer and Helen driving through Dublin for the first time. The next twelve months was to be one of the toughest and most difficult years of our lives but a successful one.

I firstly went house-hunting. When I found York House, York Road, Dun Laoghaire, it had a side garden fronting on to the road behind a tall wall. It seemed to be an opportunity similar to the site I used in Sligo, offering me a chance of repeating that success. York House was big and I planned to convert it into five apartments and to build a new house in the garden. We would live in the new house and enjoy the income from the apartments. We bought York House in September 1967 and quickly secured planning permission. For bridging finance I borrowed from Lombard Finance, manager Ken Wall, and started building the new house. We had designed it in the Mediterranean style, fitting a red-tiled roof and black shutters.

Meanwhile I had thrown myself completely into my new job and although I didn't really feel comfortable with Raymond's drinking habits, which he expected me to share, and the unnecessarily long hours, I made myself fit in and I sold boilers like they were going out of fashion. When I started my job, there were no enquiries in the pipeline. I only stayed in the job for eleven months and in that time I sold eleven steam boilers and left a promising pipeline behind me. I won the award as top sales agent in the world which carried an all-expenses trip to the States. Raymond took the award although it was my achievement. I didn't mind as I was very busy managing all that was going on

My enquiries into the fishing industry were leading to a decision. Bord Iascaigh Mhara had identified a suitable second hand trawler in France and would send an inspector to vet it and, if thought fit, would certificate it. They had found me a skipper, Paddy Bonner, in Burtonport. The deal of sharing the catch among crew and owner plus a margin for the owner to save up for a second boat was explained and was attractive.

In addition, BIM would contribute 33% of the trawler cost. The economics all added up and I was ready to make another big sideways jump. The problem was that I had all my money tied up in York House. I would need a further loan to bridge that gap. The trawler would supply the security for a 66% loan. I was referred to the Bank of Ireland in Killybegs where the manager arranged such contracts regularly. To my surprise they turned me down flat, a firm refusal to even consider us for any loan. It wasn't a matter of security, they just couldn't see us townies as successful fisherman. We didn't have a clue of what we were letting ourselves in for. Helen was relieved and today I am glad that this avenue was closed.

The winter of 1967/1968 was a difficult one for us, and especially for Helen. Living in York House with a Victorian kitchen was extremely uncomfortable, dark and cold. I was out at work for long days in the office, a 7.00 a.m. departure and home at 9.00 p.m. Having no friends and a young baby all contributed to her discomfiture. However, our new house was progressing rapidly and we would move in during 1968. We would then be able to start work converting York House into flats for our pension.

Easter was coming and we were looking forward to spending it with Ann and Aubrey Bradshaw in Sligo. Little did we suspect that our visit to Sligo would change our lives forever.

CHAPTER 8
TOP TOMS

OUR TOMATO VENTURE BEGAN while holidaying over the 1968 Easter weekend. On Easter Sunday, coming out of the church we accidentally met an old acquaintance, Joe Moss. I had known Joe from my schooldays in St Macartan's and he had been a customer of mine in Shell. He owned seven acres of land just outside Sligo and had erected a half-acre glasshouse heated by a large steam boiler. He wanted to go to Canada to grow trees, and would I buy his farm? He wanted £10,000. As I only had £5000, he would take it and let me pay the balance at £1000 per year over five years, free of interest. I would think about it. If you set out to pick a location for a tomato farm, the North West coast of Ireland is not the ideal spot, given the wind, the rain, the lack of sunshine to energise photosynthesis. Nor is it an ideal location for a nationwide waste oil collection service.

For years, I had been on the lookout for a suitable piece of land near to Dublin but without success. So, when I was offered a site in Sligo, it wasn't perfect, but entrepreneurs must be flexible, lucky and prepared to adapt every opportunity to reach their goal. This was a low-capital offer which made it possible to get into business and generate cash flow towards the prime objective, Ireland's first privately-owned oil refinery.

Driving back to Dublin on Monday night I was excited by the idea. I had a small handbook, *Grow Your Own Tomatoes* issued by the British Ministry of Agriculture, priced two shillings and sixpence (17.5p, approximately). This would teach me how to grow tomatoes. I would need to market them under a strong brand name. Channel Islands tomatoes were marketed under the name Guernsey Toms; J Arthur Rank had a catering company, Top Table, so I combined the two to name my brand Top Toms. Our company would be named Sunnyfresh Nurseries. This was all worked out in my mind by the time we reached Mullingar; the rest of the journey was focused on finance.

We are Top Toms

During the next six weeks I visited banker Ken Wall again. Our new house was nearly finished and while I would be illiquid until both properties were sold there was enough equity to arrange further bridging of £8000, enough to pay Joe together with start-up costs. At this stage I reviewed our finances and the results of our ventures to date:

Profit from Union St = £4,000. Profit from York Road = £7,000. Total = £11,000. We also had £4,000 from personal sources giving us a total of £15,000.

Some readers may not know or remember that interest rates at that time were running at 15 to 17% and even 19%. We could afford few mistakes as we sought to produce good crops and good cash flow to maintain such a charge. Yet somehow, we managed to build a business up from £15,000 to a significant value in just ten years – we were very lucky.

It was a great relief for me to resign from Clyde Fuel Systems. I was obliged to Raymond O'Flynn for prising me out of Shell, but I was still an employee, whereas I really wanted to do my own thing. We put York House up for sale and bought a small estate car which I knew I would need. We rented a detached four-bedroom house on Pearse Road and headed back to Sligo with our young family, Peter age 5 and Suzanne age 1. It was just twelve months since we had left, but what a hectic year it had been. A lot of experience, a boost of self-confidence and £7000 richer, enough to fund our first new one acre extension to the original half acre. The question was whether we could finish the new house and sell it together with York House in time to order up the new glasshouse.

Starting up a new career, I went to meet my staff of one – an old worker, Peter MacGuinn, who had worked in horticulture for many years (his wage in 1967 was £7 per week). Peter was a gentleman and my reliable supporter for some years. There would be support from a conscientious County Horticultural Adviser and an excellent technical advisor from the Department of Agriculture.

Developing a new glasshouse complex is seriously dependent on seasonality, on soil damage by construction machines and on timing, to get out the next crop. This was to be our ongoing challenge as we expanded from year to year. That summer we ordered our first glasshouse and a team arrived from Holland in October to build it. The foreman was a Dutch man, Jan Moret, who impressed me.

It didn't take long for our first crisis to hit us. At the halfway stage when the construction was at its most vulnerable, a force eight storm hit us and ripped dozens of glass sheets into the air flying like leaves, only for them to crack down and break into shards of dangerous pieces. As the sheets of glass were six feet by three feet in size they were extremely dangerous. Of course, the construction staff had been removed from the site for the duration of the storm but when the wind dropped, someone had to enter the construction site to clear the dangerous debris. I noted how the foreman Moret single-handedly cleared the site before calling in the rest of the three-man team. It was a rare challenge.

Helen and I sowed our first seeds in seed boxes in the warm spare bedroom and watched them anxiously. It was much cheaper than heating our half acre glass house. As soon as the first two baby leaves (cotyledons) appear, they must have light, so we pricked them out into pots and spread them into the glass house. One of our problems was the boiler's unreliable oil burner. Every time it switched off it would fail to start up and had to be fired up manually. We established a routine. I would relight the boiler at 6.00 p.m. and 9.00 p.m. and go to bed at 10.00 p.m. Helen would relight it at 12.00 midnight. I would relight it at 3.00 a.m. and 6:30 a.m. Relighting the boiler meant opening the huge boiler door, throwing in a lighted newspaper and pressing the restart button on the burner. It was like Dante's *Inferno*, scary and dangerous. Because of the cold nights the warm boiler house attracted many rats so we would point our headlights at the open boiler house door for a period before entering. That would scatter the rats. No job for a woman, but Helen was up for it.

The new glasshouse was being fitted out with miles of heating pipes, automated ventilation and irrigation. A new boiler house and packing shed had been built and a new boiler purchased from my previous employers Clyde Fuel Systems Ltd. As the new boiler fired up to heat the enlarged space, we were thankful that the night watch of restarting a faulty burner was ended. It really had been a worrying and most unpleasant experience.

The plants grew, the tomatoes ripened, and the business expanded. During that year, 1969, I asked Jan Moret to join me as Operations Manager. He would get 27% of the equity to be earned over the next three years if he invested £2,000. An important milestone. Jan, his wife Jeanne and young family moved to Sligo. By that time we had established good relations with a small number of fruit wholesale customers: Cyril Armstrong in Lisnaskea, Co Fermanagh; his brother Harry in Wilson's in Belfast; Devine's in Belfast; Heavey Brothers in Castlebar and Theo Burke and Tony Gray in Sligo. We also had important agents in the Dublin market.

During the following years we built up a significant business in Northern Ireland but had to be careful because of the Troubles. The Markets area in Belfast was notoriously dangerous as it was the frontline between the warring factions and was frequently the scene of gun battles.

There was little danger in delivering to Lisnaskea, just outside Enniskillen, but Belfast was another matter. Cyril Armstrong generously offered to carry our shipments up to Wilson's at no cost to us which reduced our trips to two each week to supply Devine's. One day I was unloading my van at Devine's when the salesman, Seamus, shouted, 'Down.' As I crouched beneath the stacks of fruit, I heard four gunshots in rapid succession, but nobody got hurt that day. After a few minutes, normal business resumed, and I was told that shooting like this was not unusual.

Later that year we went to see an exhibition in Holland and ordered another acre of glass which would bring us up to two and half; construction to start in June 1970.

All our glasshouse expansion was funded in the same way: 40% own funds, 30% government grant and 30% Amro Bank who were specialists in funding the huge Dutch glasshouse industry. They issued their loans based on ten promissory notes which they would present for payment six-monthly. We would require substantial bridging funds until the construction had been satisfactorily finished. Our bank manager in AIB, Sligo, was familiar with the process from the previous expansion. He knew the business was being well-managed and was comfortable with the arrangement. He promised to get the bridging finance confirmed in writing by head office, but before he could do so, all the Irish banks went on strike. Unbelievable! How can an economy survive with such malfunctions?

During the next half year, I sought him out several times. No, he couldn't talk to me, no he couldn't get approval as he was on strike, yes, I'd be all right as it was a straightforward bank-ing exercise. To run the business, we opened a bank account in Enniskillen and lodged our Northern Irish sales income there. Indeed we built up a fair deposit and earned £3,000 interest. Our Sligo and Castlerea customers paid in cash or in social welfare cheques which we accepted but couldn't cash until the strike ended. We also wrote significant cheques to our glasshouse constructors along with many other payments which would not be presented until the end. The bank manager reckoned we would be able to sort it all out after the strike.

As though we had not had enough problems, a big one erupted at the halfway stage as we waited anxiously for our huge new glasshouse to arrive. We were pleased when the Dutch agent called us from Dublin to announce its arrival into the docks. I listened to the midday news on RTE and heard the announcement that Palgrave Murphy, the leading Irish shipper, shipping agents and stevedores had called in a receiver. This was an event of national importance – a bit like the Mersey Harbour Board declaring insolvency. I was glad to hear a statement from a Minister assuring the country that the government would help. Then I had second thoughts; I had heard too many broken government promises. Sorting out a huge mess across many Irish ports would take time and surely would need a government-appointed administrator. That would take months (and in fact did), what would happen to our glass-house? Timing is critical when growing a summer crop. We must get the glasshouse closed before Christmas to allow for heating up the soil ready for planting out in March to create cash flow in June to start meeting the first promissory note. We must get the shipment cleared through customs and out of the docks before it was impounded by a receiver or administrator. I called the agent alerting him for action.

This was a new problem for me, but it had to be tackled. I gathered £500 cash and met the agent at Dublin Port. We had many invoices detailing hundreds of different items including brass, zinc, aluminium, nuts, bolts, steel bars, pipes, glass et cetera and all requiring different import duties. The agent and I queued up five times to apply for an import authority and to pay the duty. We failed five times. I was back on cigarettes by this time and the customs clerk was nearly as frustrated as we were. 'Give me something simple so that I can calculate a sensible rate of duty.' Finally, we hit on an idea and overnight the agent typed one new invoice. Just one page saying, "One glasshouse of area 4,000 m², price £20,000." We entered this invoice, it was immediately accepted, duty assessed and paid. Now to the next tricky stage.

We had arranged for five large trucks to meet us as we hoped to remove the forty-foot containers and deliver them to Sligo. We would probably be breaking the law. This was my first experience with Dublin dockers and a remarkably interesting one. The Port of Dublin was in Limbo, nothing was moving. For an hour we met nothing but disinterest. The realisation of the liquidation had shocked everyone; why work, if they would be out of a job tomorrow? We needed them to use the big four wheeled machines that could straddle a forty-foot container and deposit it on a forty-foot truck, but they were all standing idle and the drivers were sitting in a corner sulking. When I identified the apparent leader of the pack, I had a quiet word with him: £50 for him and £50 for each driver plus an extra £10 for him for each other driver he persuaded to work. When he saw the wad of notes in my hand – I didn't show it all – suddenly things began to happen. 'Quick, get those trucks in before they were stopped;" £20 to the gate keeper,' done! The five trucks queued up, the five machines were standing in a row each carrying a container, The trucks were loaded on and on the way to Sligo in less than an hour. I was home for tea after two extraordinary days. It was many years before I managed to stop smoking again.

Problem solved? It was only beginning!

The following January with the strike still running, Helen and I were at a dinner dance in Jury's hotel. While on the dance floor, the AIB bank manager said to me, 'I'm surprised to see you here – don't you know you're in trouble?' I tried to see him the next day, but the bank was still closed. I had received no communication from the bank for six months. Newspapers had reported that the strike had ended, but the banks would not open again for business for some time to sort things out. The manager would not meet me until the bank opened. When it did open, and I met him he informed me that there were two men down from head office going through all the accounts and that we were one of nine businesses in trouble. They would refuse to honour our cheques beyond the limit of the cash I could input and would return the rest. It was no use my pointing out that I was due a government grant of £8,000 and a Dutch loan of £8,000. The bridging loan had not been finalised and the new funds would not materialise until June when construction was finished; I owed £10,000 in early February. All the banks had agreed to have a grand clearing of all accounts on the following Friday, Black Friday! Unless I deposited the £10,000 by close of business on or before that day, he would send my overdrawn cheques to the bank head office for referral to drawer.

We were quite desperate not knowing what to do or where to turn. I found it difficult, but I asked a good friend to lend me £10,000 (€155,000 in 2020), a big ask. He was one of the wealthiest people in Sligo and one of the bank's best customers. I showed him the funding agreements, he believed my story and promised to lend me £10,000. It took a little manoeuvring to arrange everything as the bank manager behaved like a weasel, fretting and threatening, but we managed to do so at the last moment. It was a close call.

Eight Sligo businesses were put out of business that weekend including Inishfree Potteries, an Irish Italian ceramic factory which had a full order book. What damage that bank strike caused! The performance by the combined bank staff and boards was simply disgraceful, putting their personal interests before all others. As we proved, Sunnyfresh Nurseries was a well-run, profitable business which went on to employ perhaps a hundred people. This would have been put out of business along with the eight others by selfish, greedy Scrooges. One might conclude that a bank manager who threatens a good customer on a dancefloor is lacking more than tact. After the debacle, he tried to maintain social contacts as if we were friends. A weak man, with little backbone.

After all the excitement, we progressed through 1971 building up our staff and getting our new packing house and grading machine into operation. We were producing a good output of quality tomatoes and were getting top prices in all our markets. Our output was sixty tons per acre per crop with two crops each year. We were now quite a big nursery shipping regularly to market and a driver delivering to Belfast and to Dublin. One hot summer evening, as we packed the van for the Dublin market, I told the driver to get an early night. Our tomatoes were due in the market at 5:30 a.m. which required an early departure and I knew the driver worked part-time in a band. He promised he was not playing that night, I pressed him on the point, and he was quite definite, claiming he never played in the band when he was due to drive to market the next day. The following morning Helen had a call from the police informing us that our driver had driven into the back of a truck parked on the road. He was dead. 'Will you please inform his widow and his father?' Helen and I did so – a sad business and an incredibly sad day. Running a business means caring for your staff as much as anything else and it is truly disheartening when things go wrong in this area.

Our crop was promising a bumper yield and cashflow on target so I took pleasure re-moving our account from AIB and opening a new account in the Bank of Ireland managed by Brian O'Neill, a good move. Brian supported us for many years and became a good friend. If he had had our account in 1970, I believe the situation would have been better managed. A curious coincidence occurred many years later, when his daughter Susan and her husband John bought a house next door to our son Peter in Dulwich, south-east London. She had actually worked during her student holidays on our tomato grader. Thanks to her friendship, we were able to meet Brian again twenty-five years after the event.

As 1972 dawned the time had arrived to start on my ten-year dream of a waste oil recycling plant. We had become significant users of fuel oil, burning 200,000 gallons a year and had established a demand which, if we could supply it with low cost oil, would make us very profitable.

Developing our waste oil collection service, I used our existing Sunnyfresh staff, van and cars. One of the student part-timers had impressed me as an outstanding young man, Adrian Gallagher, focused and reliable. I persuaded him (after permission from his mother) to abandon university and make his career in Sunnyfresh. It was one of my better decisions as he made an important contribution to the success of the group, became a shareholder and in time became Managing Director. It was clear that we needed more management to allow Jan and I to focus on this new venture; it was time to find a real growing expert.

Our output had grown to sixty-five tons per acre, but a specialist horticulture manager was needed to drive it to seventy-five tons. We decided to seek such a grower and to add another acre of glass to carry the extra overheads. Advertising widely in the trade magazines, we met and employed Bill Dray, a stoic Sussex man who had been foreman in the UK Glasshouse Crops Research Institute in Littlehampton, Sussex. He and his wife Valerie, with their two children, sold up in England and bought a house in Sligo where they settled in quickly and were soon well-established. Bill brought a lot of know-how and innovation to the enterprise and soon improved our already good crop regimes increasing output and quality.

As Bill took over the Nursery, Jan and I started the engineering programme to erect a basic oil recycling plant. I bought a second-hand tanker ex-Gulf Oil in Belfast. It had been crashed and had a twisted chassis, so my brother-in-law, Brian Raftery, named it the 'Crab'. At this stage, Adrian and I canvassed enough large garages to start up a collection service. I organised a card index system to plan collections which Adrian administered and while he continued telesales, I drove the tanker to Dublin myself and started collections. Having learned the ropes, I then employed a driver and trained him.

The following year was a year for consolidation. Bill Dray added expertise, the nursery blossomed while Jan continued with construction and engineering. He built a large boiler house which contained two large Clyde boilers, leaving room for another even bigger boiler to heat the extra glasshouse which we were planning. We had a particularly good crop that year and our cash position stage strengthened. This encouraged us to plan another 1¼ acre of glass which would bring our coverage to almost four acres. We decided to figure to visit Holland in the New Year, 1974 to negotiate its purchase, which would cost £Ir25,000, (€220,000 in 2020).

The world was suddenly shocked in October 1973 by the unexpected attack on Israel by Syria and Egypt. From October 6-25 they fought and in spite of assistance from Iran, the Arabs failed, and Israel had another victory. The effect on oil prices was dramatic as it shot up from $3 to $11 per barrel in a few weeks. We were glad to have our own supply of low-cost fuel. We weren't to know that the new regime of high oil prices was just beginning. It would have a profound effect on our business in the future.

As our tomato vans were not needed for deliveries during winter, we used them for staff to travel around the country delivering empty oil barrels into the smaller garages to promote storage of their waste oil. One November evening, Adrian called me from Dundalk to say our new Ford van had just been stolen from outside his hotel; the IRA had needed it for a 'job'.

A few days later we got a call from the police sergeant in Hackballs Cross, a village on the Irish border. Our van was there but not mobile, it had been severely damaged. Jan and I took another van and went to tow it home. As we approached the scene accompanied by the police, we learned what had happened. The IRA had not damaged it and had used it only as a potential booby trap on a road which they wanted closed. In fact, when the Irish Army examined it, it was innocent of any bombs or any interference. The army was accompanied by a film crew from a Canadian Broadcasting company who had seen no excitement on their trip and needed something dramatic to show the folks back home.

The Irish Army obliged and put three rockets through our van leaving no glass and huge holes in the front, back and sides – a sorry sight. The car vultures had arrived soon afterwards and stripped out the engine but it had wheels and brakes and could be steered so we towed it home. The insurance settlement was pathetic, and we lost several thousand pounds in the incident.

In January 1974, we were finalising our plans to visit Holland. We would be looking for a substantial loan from Amro Bank, so we prepared all our files showing our strong financial position. I included the Irish Government's offer of an 30% grant. Together these should be enough to gain the bank's continuing support. Jan and I would go together, but Helen would like a trip to Holland and decided to come too. When Valerie Dray realised we were travelling through Kent, she took a lift to visit her parents there.

We were driving my new Hillman Hunter KEI63 and, carrying four of us, it was a really full car as we set out for Holland.

It was to be a memorable trip.

CHAPTER 9
THE WRONG PLACE AT THE WRONG TIME

As I LINED UP my car preparing to board the Liverpool ferry to Dublin we were approached by twelve tough-looking man.

'Get out of the car, you're all coming with us,' they ordered.

We were confused and started to ask questions

'What about the car?' we asked.

'We will look after the car,' they replied.

'We'll miss our ferry,' we argued.

'Yes, you will …'

Our trip to the Westland of Holland had gone well. We had ordered a fifty thousand square-foot glass house for delivery in the autumn and secured the financial support of Amro Bank, for 30% funding of the £Ir25,000 contract (€220,000 in 2020), the third time they had supported us. Our glass houses would exceed four acres.

Heading back to Ostend, Jan was driving; it was early February and a huge storm was raging in the English Channel. We were due on the Liverpool ferry that night but everything that could go wrong did go wrong, an astonishing series of coincidences which put us in harm's way.

The crossing was the worst I had ever experienced and when we tried to tie up in Folkestone it became quite dangerous. The deck master was determined to tie up and discharge the cargo of cars. We were the first vehicle in line to exit and when the mooring lines were at last secured the unloading bridge went down, the green light went on for disembarking. The ship was see-sawing down and up to six feet from the ramp and Jan wouldn't attempt to drive off. Just then a mooring line broke and the ferry swung away from the dock. Finally, the ship put out to sea again and sailed up to Dover where we docked safely.

As we went through Customs the officer asked us to open the boot. We couldn't! This was the first of the coincidences. The car was almost new, but for no reason and for the first time, the key would not turn in the lock. As all the other cars drove out of the Customs shed we stood around wondering what to do. When I suggested using a crowbar to lever it open the officer thought that was too much and let us go on our way.

By this time, we were running seriously behind time and had agreed to collect Valerie at a roundabout on the Dover road. The wind was almost at storm force with driving rain and poor visibility. This was before mobile phones, and running late it proved difficult to collect Valerie who we knew was waiting. She had sought some shelter and we drove around the large roundabout with flashing lights and blowing horns until we were able to collect her. We were still trying for the Liverpool ferry, but by the time we cleared London realised that we couldn't. We were tired and relieved to find a small comfortable roadside hotel where we could stay the night. We had to borrow a crowbar from the landlord who helped Jan to force open the boot to access our luggage. Later we went across the road to the local pub for dinner, followed by several Irish coffees which became a topic for pleasant conversation.

The weather had cleared by morning and we headed north. There seemed to be extra police activity as we saw police with binoculars on two of the bridges crossing the motorway.

At this stage we had not heard that the nation was on high alert after a shocking bomb explosion, leaving a number of people killed and seriously injured in a privately-hired bus carrying air force personnel and their families from Manchester back to their base in Catterick. This had happened on 4 February and was followed by another bomb in the Thames Valley on 12 February, close by where we were staying. We didn't realise that the police were looking for us.

I had previously agreed to call in to Rugby to meet a friend who had an oil recycling business, so we detoured for a couple of hours and then made our way cross country until we reached Liverpool. We were early so we went looking for a restaurant and parked near the Liver Building. After a good dinner and lots of wine we came back to the car. Valerie spotted an identity card lying on the ground. It looked important so I put it in the front glove compartment to bring it back to Sligo for posting to Liverpool.

The following twenty-four hours were probably one of the worst experiences of our lives.

It was at this point we were apprehended with the ominous instruction, 'You're coming with us,' by twelve armed Special Branch Officers. Each of us were led off by three men, placed in separate cars and taken by different routes to the main Liverpool Bridewell where they continued to keep us apart while we were signed in by the Desk Sergeant. The offender who was signed in before us was up on a charge of peeing against the door of Liverpool Cathedral. We were informed that we were being held under the Merseyside and Docks Provision Act of 1848 and, importantly, we were not charged.

We were all thoroughly searched; Helen was particularly upset by the intimacy of her body search by a butch policewoman.

All this time, no one would talk to us or tell us why we were being held. We were taken separately to offices on the sixth floor of the Liverpool Police headquarters where we sat on chairs all night and most of the next day. We each had one or two officers in our room at all times. I kept up a barrage of questions. Each hour on the hour I demanded to know why we were being held, but nobody would tell me. We were all closely interviewed and we gave a full description of everything we had done and why. To say we were upset would not describe how we felt. I felt angry, bewildered and worried. We had nothing to occupy ourselves. Helen was given *Woman's Weekly* magazine (awful) and she smoked sixty cigarettes that night. I was luckier and had an old *Readers Digest* which helped to pass the time. I got a pen and paper and listed out a number of questions I wanted answered.

There were no refreshments available and when I asked for breakfast, they offered to go out for sandwiches provided that I paid, as they had no budget for feeding people in what were their offices. I paid again for lunch and for cigarettes so by the time I arrived back in Dublin I had run out of cash. The other three didn't know that I was paying and thought that the police were providing the food.

We could almost judge how the investigation was proceeding by the demeanour of our captors. By 3.00 a.m. they were beginning to relax a little and look less angry, but then suddenly it changed and attitudes became more hostile. What had happened to change things?

Early in the morning as dawn broke, I looked out of the window to see several large black Jaguar cars arriving. As the morning dragged on several senior looking men would look into my room and stare thoughtfully at me as though thinking, 'do I know you?' This was getting weird. At one point I approached the window to look out and was abruptly pulled back by my minders. Did they think I might jump out? 'No, but there are forty telescopic cameras focussed on this window. Don't show your face unless you want to see yourself on the front of every paper in Europe tomorrow.' I later sneaked a quick peep and saw a barrage of cameras – scary. The word was out that the Catterick bombers were being held here! It was a pan-European story.

Helen and I were anxious about our children and knew that all our families would be worrying at our not arriving home. At the time of our release Helen was allowed one phone call. Her minder stared into her face as she spoke to Catherine Raftery, monitoring what she said very closely. Helen told Catherine that we were being held by the police in Liverpool and if we weren't home in twenty-four hours to inform Minister Ray MacSharry. Would she also inform Valerie's husband Bill and Nurse Shannon who was looking after baby Sinéad? Our younger children, Michael and Suzanne, were staying with Catherine, while Peter was next door in John and Celine Shea's. Catherine had seen the main item on the Irish TV news, that a young Irish couple, a Dutch man and an English woman were being held in Liverpool, but hadn't made the connection until Helen's call.

The ordeal ended when a Chief Inspector came in to tell us that we had been cleared and would be on the night ferry to Dublin. The four of us were re-united as he explained all that happened.

We had been suspects for both the Catterick and the Thames Valley bombs – why? Here is the story.

The police had been on high alert looking for an IRA cell which included a dark-haired woman (Helen) and a Dutch man (Jan), then another bomb was set off in a military establishment – a Naval Academy close to where we had slept the night in Buckinghamshire. When an Irish car was seen driving north (fleeing from the scene), the balloon went up. The computer indicated that we had entered the country but had not opened our boot (the bomb was in there). The Buckinghamshire bomb had gone off at a time which suited our overnight location. Our movements may have allowed us to place the bomb while building up an alibi by dining and visiting the pub. When the police decided to stop us on the motorway, we eluded capture by leaving the road after spotting the police (so they deduced).

Against that, we appeared to be normal business people. I had repeatedly referred them to our business files which showed a genuine business record. I had also asked them to contact the Bishop and Ray MacSharry to confirm our bona fides. Yes – but were these the real Helen and Fred Duffy? The police had to investigate each and every detail.

First, the locked boot: the Kent police met the Customs Officer to investigate while Thames Valley police met the hotelier. Had it really been necessary to crowbar it? Had the hotelier seen the contents? Yes, he had.

Second, the alibi: Thames Valley police met the locals in the pub to determine the possibility of one of us slipping off to fix the bomb.

Third, the detour off the M1: My waste oil friend in Rugby was visited by the East Midlands police to confirm my story and identity.

Finally, the last straw, and the reason why people became so hostile to us. Just when they were beginning to accept that we were who we said we were and not bombers, they found a most incriminating document in the glove compartment of the car. The identity card which Valerie had found lying on the ground was for a senior Mersey Docks inspector, authorising the bearer to go anywhere in the dock area. Worse still, he looked like me, if I had worn glasses. That explained the staring men.

As both Valerie and I confirmed how she had found it on the ground they had to confirm that the rightful owner had lost it in that particular car park. As luck would have it that man was playing rugby in north Lancashire, so a fast car was rushed up-country to find him. Yes, he had lost it yesterday and yes, he had parked in the Liver Building car park.

The Inspector informed us that we had presented a big challenge to the police forces across England. Quite early on, they thought that we were innocent, but they had to prove that all the coincidences were just that. Where to hold us – they couldn't put us in gaol, or we'd all have a criminal record. As there were no bed facilities, why not put us in a hotel? How could they secure it? Already there were over twenty detectives guarding us. The staff in the offices we occupied had been given the day off! Why no food? As an office building, it had a kettle but no cooked food, and no budget for buying food as we were a one-off. Why not contact our friends in Sligo? They had done so. Sligo police had visited Bill Dray to confirm that his wife was who she said she was, and had called to our house to confirm that we were away. They had wanted to clear us as quickly as possible and they had used all their resources, Kent, Thames Valley, East Midlands, Yorkshire and Lancashire police forces. The Inspector told us that it was the biggest investigation he knew of, as more than eighty police and three Chief Constables were involved, driving all over the country.

As I continued my own angry questioning, he told us that he was holding the Dublin ferry for us but couldn't hold it for much longer. Deciding that we had heard enough, our car was already aboard and the keys were in the purser's office. The paparazzi were all around the building hoping to photograph us when we were moved and the police were anxious to help us avoid this. We four would squeeze into a little yellow Mini, to be driven by a policeman. The ship's officers had been primed to close up the ramp as soon as we were aboard. It all went according to plan. The mini roared up the ramp, did a U-turn, dropped us and left. The ramp came up and we began to feel safe. The ship's officers brought us up to the reception desk where we were expected but as we turned to go to our cabins a cameraman approached us. I went a little mad – pushed Helen and Valerie into a ladies' loo and jumped for the camera, shouting and ready to kill him while trying to cover my face. The reporter was hustled away. We learned afterwards that he was from the *Liverpool Echo* and obviously had a pal in the police who had told him what was happening. Apparently, the *Echo* liked to use the ship's lounges during the day for fashion shows and other PR events. The captain telephoned the editor and threatened to withdraw all privileges if a picture had been taken and printed. In my opinion, no picture was taken; certainly none appeared. Since that occurrence I can empathise with anyone who forcibly objects to a camera poked in their face.

When we arrived back in Sligo there was no fuss and no apparent general knowledge of our mishap. Helen had been a day overdue in the hospital and some of her medical colleagues seem to have known something, but nothing was said and Helen was so traumatised she couldn't talk about it, and even still has difficulty. Curiously, one of her first patients was the father of a local convicted IRA man who said, 'Glad to know you got out safely.' How did he know? We were all traumatised by the experience; it was the shock of the total disruption of our lives into a world where we were suspected of being mass murderers.

Reviewing the situation, this was potentially the most dangerous event in our lives as we might well have finished up in goal for twenty or more years. This was 1974, the year which led to the wrongful conviction of the Guildford Four and the Maguire Seven. Both groups served fifteen or sixteen years in prison until their cases were quashed and three police officers charged with conspiracy to prevent the course of justice. In 1970, the Birmingham Six were wrongfully convicted and spent seventeen years in prison, until the case was squashed in 1991 and Superintendent George Reade and two other police charged with perjury.

Sadly, in 1974 Judith Ward was convicted for the Catterick bomb and spent eighteen years in jail before her case was judged to have been unlawful and she was released. Four cases, all occurring in 1974, were wrongly, and some criminally, convicted, leading to lengthy and unfair times in jail.

We were fortunate that we were investigated at quite extraordinary speed and efficiency in an exemplary performance of good police work. It was a praiseworthy achievement by the police to prove our innocence in a complex series of coincidences in a remarkably short period.

As a businessman, I sent two bills to the Merseyside police authority. The first was for expenses – food consumed during the investigation, the extra dinner on the ferry including the wine; the extra cost of hiring Nurse Shannon, in all it came to about £50. I also sent an account for my professional services at £25/hour for assisting the police in their enquiries. I got back an amusing letter with a cheque for the £50, but a refusal for my services.

No one has ever been convicted in connection with the Catterick or Buckinghamshire bombs.

CHAPTER 10
ATLAS OIL

THE SUCCESS OF ATLAS Oil was always going to be influenced by the price of crude oil. Following the unsuccessful attack on Israel by Syria and Egypt during the Jewish Yom Kippur festival in 1973, the price of oil shot up from $3 to $11 a barrel. This was an unprecedented price hike, sending the world economy tumbling but putting a smile on our faces.

The oil price was to continue rising year on year, helping us to grow our business. Having started from scratch in a small, self-built oil reclamation plant on our tomato farm in Sligo, we continued to operate from there for many years. Our two trucks would set off across Ireland collecting waste oil from Donegal to Kerry, using a planned collection schedule based on the storage capacity of the supplier.

Given the diverse nature of the Irish economy this type of operation was the key to a highly successful collection industry. Large five thousand-gallon tankers were routed on two-, three-, or even four-day runs into the rural areas, while smaller two thousand-gallon tankers were used for city work. Drivers were heavily incentivised to fill the last 10% of the tanker. Recovering from the excitement in Liverpool, we were busy. There was a lot to do in both sections of the business which were expanding. Spring is a busy time in the protected glasshouse crops industry. Plants had to be spaced out into two and a half acres of glass. In addition, we were preparing for the arrival in September of another acre and a quarter, which would bring our total under-glass to over four acres, requiring 250,000 gallons of oil per year.

One of the Northern Ireland fleet

Our ten-year plan was coming to fruition. We had the launch pad for our main objective. But we had more! We had a strong cash flow which would support the considerable expenditure expected to develop the Atlas programme. The changeover from Shell to Atlas recycled oil would be a gradual one, reducing our costs from the beginning. We had used the last eighteen months improving our recycling facility. It wasn't perfect but it was producing a combustible fuel.

One Friday afternoon, I received a call from my old fuel oil manager, Frank McArdle. Could I drop into Irish Shell House to meet the Shell MD, Bernard Nolan, to discuss the situation? Our meeting went politely, until Nolan suggested that he could easily put out us out of business if so minded. This of course had been expected, and was easily countered. Our position was that Atlas Oil had a finite supply of product restricted to what could be collected in Ireland. We would insist on selling that small amount and if Shell took this business from us, we would repeatedly move to other outlets, causing Shell to drop price across a wide number of customers. In view of the small quantity we would have, this seemed reasonable to Shell and we parted amicably.

What I didn't tell him was that we were just establishing ourselves in Northern Ireland and were buying two small coastal tankers to uplift contaminated oils from the oil refinery in Milford Haven and from tank bottoms from oceangoing tankers.

It was around this time that I changed the company name to Atlas Waste Oil and thought up the slogan, 'Don't dump it, we'll pump it'.

During that year I was adjudicated the winner of the 'Award for Business Enterprise', to be presented by Mr Tom O'Donnell, Minister for Agriculture. An all-male affair, there had been some question of my wife attending but I soon sorted that out.

Meanwhile, we had launched an aggressive thrust into Northern Ireland where a competitor had established a small plant in Caledon, Co Tyrone. Our launch was successful and in June 1975 we bought out our competitor, Northern Lubricants. We offered the owner, Archie Dobell, a small equity share and a Directorship, but he refused and retired back to Wales.

Bill Dray was fully managing the Sligo nursery. I asked him to supervise the oil business, routing the trucks and processing the waste oil. I transferred Jan Moret to the growing operation in Caledon, as well as a junior foreman, Eugene Martin. They shared the living accommodation with Adrian Gallagher, my young Sales Manager, and me.

Following the initiative of Dr Ken Whitaker, the continuing programme of economic expansion was being well managed by the Industrial Development Authority, IDA, which focused on attracting inward investment. Reacting to the high cost of oil and its resultant pressure on the national economy, the Authority readily met an entrepreneurial salesman, Basil Rossi, who had an agency for the Meinken patented oil refining process. Rossi tried to sell it to the IDA, who referred him to Cement Roadstone Holdings, one of the largest fleet operators in Ireland and a company looking for diversification.

The chairman of Cement Roadstone was Tom Roche, a successful entrepreneur who had started a sand and gravel business driving one truck and built it into a nationwide supplier of surface coverings. His son-in-law – Dan Tierney, himself a successful businessman, seeking to build a portfolio of investments – heard of the enquiry and contacted the IDA. At that time, we had been expanding our business for three years and were operating a nationwide service. I was in bed with pneumonia when a call came from the IDA to attend a meeting the following morning in Tierney's office to discuss the IDA support for a Tierney/Atlas Oil plant using the Meinken process. 'Too bad about being sick, but if you aren't at the meeting you'll be left out of the picture.' Tough talk! I went to Dublin by train and met Basil Rossi, Dan Tierney, a CRH representative and IDA personnel. I was nervous and concerned, as until then I had no knowledge of any re-refining process designed to produce lubricating oil. I sat in the meeting realising how totally ignorant I was but careful not to show it.

Used lube oil contains a number of impurities, carbon and water from the hydro-carbon combustion process, burnt chemicals components in the oil, some diesel or petrol diluents, atmospheric dust introduced into the engine from the atmosphere and of course dirt picked up in the service garages. Our small business was based on the premise that most of the contaminants could be removed by settling tanks, draining the water from the bottom and filtration. Powerful centrifuges would later prove more effective than filters in removing the solids. This process produced a combustible fuel of uncertain calorific value, to which we added some diesel oil. Our own experience in burning 200,000 gallons annually had taught us a great deal on reducing the water content, but at this stage we were still learning on the job while making good profits.

I was informed that some, but not all, European Governments regarded burning waste oil as wasteful and environmentally unacceptable when it could be re-refined back to lube oil, a more valuable product. The IDA, of course, knew less than me about re-refining against reclamation, but was interested in job creation and helping to create a new sustainable industry which would assist in the balance of payments.

I was now facing a dilemma which would challenge me for the next five years. I had to define what was the most commercial and environmental recycling process for our Irish scale of operation and at the same time, if we were to receive IDA financial support, to persuade them that we had the best process from the various points of view. I also had to become expert in the various methodologies and to be seen to be researching these while looking for potential partners or sources of technology transfer. Over the next few years, I was to travel extensively and examine many interesting technologies.

My first trip was in 1976 with Dan Tierney and a CRH engineer to Hanover to meet Dr. Meinken and Basil Rossi – very informative – then to a Meinken plant in Vermoos, Switzerland. Soon afterwards, the IDA introduced me to Berndt Haberland, a German re-refiner. We discussed a joint venture and I hosted him to dinner in Glendalough. When I visited his plant in Germany it was a huge, smelly, dirty plant, a process totally unsuitable for Ireland.

All these plants had a process that required the use of sulphuric acid to take out the contaminants from the waste oil, leaving a dark base lubricant which could be clarified and 'polished' by filter presses. Apart from being an expensive plant, the process left a toxic waste, an acid tar, which was virtually impossible to dispose of. Haberland had dug a vast reservoir, about half the size of a football field with an impervious lining. He put the acid tar into barrels and buried these in lime in the pit. When questioned about how long it would be before the acid burned through the steel barrel and through the pit lining, he didn't know. I visited a Meinken plant in Düsseldorf, again the acid tar problem. I was to find that acid tar was a problem in every Meinken plant. I couldn't imagine how we would get planning permission to operate such a system. We next visited Dr Manfred Fuchs plant in Mannheim and found a unit in pristine condition but mainly confined to bespoke laundering, not suitable.

Checking the quality

During these years I was meeting various officials to find a suitable location for our proposed reclamation plant. I met the County Managers of Monaghan and Cavan, Meath and Louth, looked at sites in Carrickmacross, Dundalk and Kingscourt, Trim and Drogheda. The CRH management in Drogheda offered me the huge quarry in Drogheda while the IDA brought me to many of their sites in the area.

One Sunday night a grim Jan Moret called to my house in Sligo giving me bad news. Apparently one of our drivers returning to Caledon with a load of waste oil had left a valve open and we had contaminated the river. We had a friendly neighbour, Sam Oliver, who had telephoned the bad news to Jan. One of his horses had been fatally poisoned. I had a difficult meeting on Monday morning but restored relations by offering to work for full compensation from our insurers. The horse had become a promising top racehorse! It took many months before the claim was successfully settled, during which time Sam and I became quite friendly over several meals in his house. Sam was a champion clay pigeon shot. His green championship blazer was covered by so many winner badges sewn on that he was on his second blazer, already half-covered. He had been selected to shoot for the Irish team in the forthcoming Olympics. He had also been selected to represent Northern Ireland in the Commonwealth Games in Montreal. He had to choose between the two. For political reasons he had no option but to shoot for Northern Ireland, although his preference was the other.

To improve our production processes, we needed to install centrifuges and I had located some second hand ones in an oil recycling plant in Glasgow. Jan Moret and I went there and met the owner, a bland pleasant older gentleman. We bought two centrifuges and I got the impression that the vendor might be open to sell his business. I planned to buy it many years later.

All this time I was getting heavily involved in the international oil recycling business, building up contacts through the trade associations, the IDA and the oil industry generally. Attending an oil reclamation conference in Cambridge, I met two of my old friends from earlier days, one a BP man and the other working for Esso. They suggested that I should be a member of the Institute of Petroleum and proceeded to nominate me. Because I was chairman of an oil company, I was elected a Fellow of the Institute.

As part of my PR build-up of Atlas, wishing to increase our stature, I applied to join the European Union of Independent Lubricant Manufacturers, UEIL. After suitable presentations I was elected to the Presidium of the Union which had direct negotiating skills with the European Commission. I have no doubt that the knowledge and prestige this membership gave Atlas contributed to our success with the IDA.

I was further invited to read a paper to the second UEIL European Congress held in Paris. I was interested to note that a paper written by Dr La France, an EEC delegate to the German Association ATIEZ, described the Atlas Oil process. At this Congress, I was approached by two delegates from Shell International: 'Would I consider a joint operation in Senegal?' but I had my hands full and wasn't interested.

On a social note my wife Helen accompanied me to the Congress Dinner for a glitzy reception by Jacques Chirac, then Mayor of Paris, at the Hotel de Ville. It was an event to remember.

William O'Brien had not forgotten the business he lost to us in collecting waste oil and was making his presence felt by having the IDA include him in the evaluation for a grant. He was pressing that his organisation was the one to build a refinery although he had no background in industrial fuel marketing, lubrication and other details which would prove helpful in managing the plant. We met jointly in the presence of the IDA and privately in discussions promoted by the IDA. I discussed the possibility of equity participation, but Mr O'Brien was not interested.

Our business was continuing to expand on both sides of the border but Northern Ireland was continuing to be a dangerous area in which to operate a fleet of oil tankers. The short, so-called "IRA Truce" ended in February 1976 when ten Protestant workers were killed that month in Bessbrook, just a few miles from Caledon. IRA prisoners would no longer get special category status as paramilitaries and would be treated as common criminals to be confined in the new Maze Prison H Blocks.

We were under considerable stress, especially at night in the isolated country house where we all lived. But we just had to get on with it. The army and police kept us informed before expected 'hot' days, anniversaries of previous occurrences. We would keep our trucks off the roads on such days.

Dr Meinken had recommended that we might modify a plant he had installed at the Transvaal Oil Refinery in Boksburg, Johannesburg. The managing director and lubricant technologist was Percy von Knoblauch, former lubricants manager for Mobile Deutschland. We contacted them and received a warm welcome together with an offer of cooperation and technical technology transfer. In March 1978 Helen and I flew there as their guests to study their adaptation of the process. It was our first time in a jumbo jet and our first visit to South Africa.

As part of our research, we brought some used oil samples with us for analysis and for the chemist's opinion on recycling them. Fourteen oils in pint jars in a soft holdall. At check-in there was little security and I was allowed to carry them to the departure lounge where I again asked permission to bring them with me. The pilot came out to us, heard our story and allowed me to carry them on board provided I placed the bag beside me.

Unimaginable today.

It was a very exciting and productive visit. Percy and his wife Rosevitha were preparing to leave South Africa and settle in Zug in Switzerland. They would take all their money with them and leave the re-refinery to their son Ralph. Percy wanted to establish and maintain contacts in Europe, partly as a possible bolt hole for his son if South Africa blew up. We left Percy with a verbal agreement that he would let me have a drawing for those parts of the plant that I wanted. I would pay him a commission based on our oil output.

During 1978 I was putting all the details in place preparing for a future reclamation plant and was in discussions with leading Irish engineers and with the Industrial Credit Corporation. The IDA had sent one of their technical staff to visit the Transvaal

Oil Refinery and was impressed. I brought a lubricant chemist from Lubrizol, Derbyshire, to Ireland on a 'get to know you' visit. He was a potential recruit for our future plant.

In this period Jan and I visited several more plants in mainland Europe, one in Basel, another in Germany and two in the UK, including a Castrol laundering plant in Glasgow. I was beginning to formulate a plan which would meet the IDA requirements as well as our own.

I hired a mechanical engineer, Joe Watson. He would be our project manager. He joined us in November 1978 and immediately began training and learning my ideas what we needed to design and construct.

The year 1979 was to be a crunch year for me; I had to:

- Find a suitable site somewhere in Ireland
- Get planning permission
- Get IDA grant support
- Build a management team to run a re-refinery
- Make hard decisions regarding Sunnyfresh Nurseries.

Searching for sites we visited Bailieboro and Ardee, thought we had decided on Drogheda, then switched to Naas. We were promised planning permission by the Kildare County Manager and had bought houses in Naas before the permission was overridden (in secrecy) by Dublin County Council, who were concerned that the River Liffey might be contaminated.

The refusal was dated 12 September 1979 and led to a series of meetings with the County Manager seeking a solution. We were quietly pointed to County Laois who had indicated a warm reception. We initiated discussions in September and our civil engineering consultant Harry O'Connell from Cavan submitted a planning application in October for a site in the

Clonminam Industrial Estate in Port Laoise. Some of the county officials were understandably nervous at the prospect of a 'refinery' in their town. To settle their fears, I hired an air taxi from Iona Airways and flew the County Manager, the Chairman of Laois County Council, the County Engineer and the Environmental Officer to the U.K. We flew to Glasgow to visit a Castrol laundering plant, then down to Birmingham to visit the Midland Oil Refinery which was located in a residential area. They were satisfied with what they saw, and we got our PP in early February and bought the site in March 1980.

Securing the full support of the IDA was a difficult matter as another firm was competing for their favours, A company with a well-established tank sludge vacuum fleet was offering a national service. This competitor owed us no favours as we had taken their garage waste oil collection, by replacing their tanks with ours and offering a free collection service *and* paying for the oil where garages had previously been charged £15 for every collection visit.

Our support from Percy von Knoblauch had been positive and together had agreed the process suitable for the Irish economy, and the strategy to secure IDA support. He had provided the necessary drawing which Joe Watson and Harry O'Connell had used in preparing our refinery layout for planning purposes and for IDA perusal. We submitted our formal application for grant support to the IDA on 25 June and our team of Joe Watson and Jan Moret went to Johannesburg on 11 August for three weeks training.

❖

One Sunday evening in late August I was having dinner with friends John and Kathleen Lyons when the phone rang. Helen answered it and spoke for a few minutes. When she came back, she told me that Percy von Knoblauch was on the telephone. When I spoke with him, I found him concerned and unusually annoyed.

'I thought you told me that you were the largest oil collector in Ireland and that you expected the support of the IDA.'

Surprised, I answered all his questions; there had been no misleading statements or false claims. Atlas had almost the entire waste oil collection business and the IDA seemed satisfied with our position.

'Then why did I receive a call from the representative of the company called William O'Brien, claiming that they were the leading waste collectors and they would get the government's support? Also, they want me to act as their consultant.'

Returning to the dinner party I referred to the conversation to which John Lyons advised, 'That's an inside job, you'd better take action.'

I of course reported this to the IDA, and to several of my contacts in the government. TOR, Transvaal Oil Refinery, is a small private company trading only in South Africa. It was clear that our competitor had seen our application to the IDA, as otherwise there was no way he could have identified this company out of the many in the world with whom we might have been partnered.

Some time later, I was informed that the Atlas Oil file had been barred to a number of IDA directors. This didn't stop our competitor, who continued to chase the von Knoblauchs and met the son, Ralph, in Manchester, asking him to act as a consultant. They were, rebuffed, but it left Von Knoblauch confused and disillusioned about the Irish scene.

The crux of the matter was whether to burn waste oil or refine it. Our competitor was only prepared to burn it, while we offered a process which combined laundering, refining and part burning. This carried the day and on 22 February 1980 we received notice of approval for a 30% capital grant. The European Investment Bank had approved an application for the Industrial Credit Corporation to support the project.

Capitalisation would be as follows:

Atlas Oil: Share capital, fixed assets and retained earnings: £399,000

IDA grant: £301,500
ICC loan: £310,000
Total: £1,009,000 (€4.2M in 2020)

A big deal in 1980.

As life continued, we had to make some difficult decisions regarding Sunnyfresh Nurseries.

The price of crude oil had continued to rise through 1974, '75, and '76. As OPEC aggressively reduced volume on 31 December 1979, the price increased from $12 per barrel to $21 and continued rising to $34 and even to $40. We had separated our accounting for the tomato business and the oil business, which in 1979 showed that the nursery was being heavily supported by low cost oil which would fetch more profit if sold to others.

It should be remembered that I had started the tomato farm mainly to create a captive customer for an oil recycling business and not, as some thought, the other way around. The venture had served its purpose. It was time to move on. Bill was asked to dismantle the glass houses and sell the glass.

The phrase 'It's better to be born lucky than rich,' came to mind when I was approached by a respected local builder Bernard Mullen, who wanted to buy the Sunnyfresh land – about seven acres – to build residential houses. I had bought the land because there was a glasshouse on it, not because it was near Sligo. It was just within the borough boundary and suitable for a residential development. I agreed with Bernard on a price that allowed him a margin for a large development. The funds would help pay for the refinery.

Having received a 'go' from all parties in Port Laoise, we employed a local builder, Vincent Ennis, and arranged for Desmond O'Malley, Minister for Industry, Commerce and Energy, to cut the first sod. A new chapter in our lives had opened and would be played out in Port Laoise.

The next two years passed quickly as we sought to develop our sales, construct the plant and expand our presence. Bob Cutler was an old contact in Lubrizol, and he joined us in January 1980, and in July I brought him and Joe Watson to oil plants in the UK and Germany.

We made a return visit to the Hamburg plant, owned by one of my friends from the UEIL, Dr Hans Koehn. Hans was a big man with a gentle kind personality. At the age of sixteen he had wanted to be a doctor and spent a few months in medical school before he was conscripted into the German army and sent to the Russian front where he was captured. The prisoners of war had no access to medical support, so when a fellow prisoner got appendicitis, Hans, because of his few months' medical background, was forced to operate on him. Armed only with a kitchen knife and no anaesthetic he performed a number of operations, losing some but saving some. As the war ended, he was ejected from the camp and left on his own. With no money and no food, he walked across war-torn Europe until he reached his home. When he told his father he wanted to be a doctor he was ordered to study engineering as Germany needed engineers to rebuild the country. Despite his success, he still regretted that decision.

During this period, I was invited to join the Environmental Committee of the Confederation of Irish Industry and represented the CII on many occasions. I was invited to give a number of talks on what makes an entrepreneur. I lectured in SFADCO (Shannon Free Airport Corporation) and to the Annual Vocational School conference in Dublin University as well as many smaller venues.

We had opened an office in Cork with a splash and were talking to other operators in the oil business, Bob Davitt of Curran Oils in Cardiff, British Railways Lubricant division, Campus Oil and many more.

Bill Dray had done a good job clearing the Sunnyfresh site of glass and steel and had taken over management of the Caledon Oil plant which was handling a large volume of oil. When he started house-hunting in Armagh he was shocked to be asked if he was Catholic or Protestant, as that would determine where he should live!

Tensions were running high in Northern Ireland. The IRA prisoners demanded to be treated as political prisoners and were in confrontation with Thatcher, then started a hunger strike in 1980, called it off for a short period, then restarted it on 1 March 1981 led by Bobby Sands. He and nine other Republican prisoners would starve themselves to death before the protest ended on 3 October.

During that period Bill Dray was finding it difficult. He was getting anonymous phone calls calling him a British bastard. His nerve broke and he asked to be taken off the job. I moved him down to Portlaoise and went up myself. As soon as I arrived, I started receiving similar calls, but this time I was called a Fenian bastard and got three specific death threats. I was glad to get a call from the Unionist MP Harold McCusker supporting me and saying that if they intended to kill me, they wouldn't phone! The army and RUC were all over the place.

I then got a call informing me that every business in the Valley must close on a certain day in support of the hunger strikers and that I must close. I took the position that Atlas Oil was in business and not in politics. I informed the caller and our staff that we would remain open. The army became active and a young captain helicoptered in several times. He left the decision on closing to me but offered an army flak jacket.

This wasn't feasible for several reasons. Firstly, I could not be seen to be wearing a British Army jacket. Secondly, if there was a bomb a flak jacket wouldn't make much difference. Interestingly, they knew the identity of the caller. It was a woman pretending to be a man with a deep voice. They were tapping her phone illegally but could not charge her under existing law.

I had been warned that there was a bomb in tank no. 5 which would be set off remotely at 11.00 a.m. if the plant was not shut down. I announced my intention to continue working and I would send a message down the valley to that effect.

All our tanks were vertical and thirty feet high. The only point of ingress for a bomb would be through a manhole on the top. To climb to the top, there was only one steel ladder, attached to tank no 1. An inspection clearly established that the encrusted dirt had not been disturbed. No one had climbed that ladder in months. I went to the top and closely examined the

1½" nuts on each manhole; again they were definitely undisturbed. We conducted a thorough search of the surrounding yard and found nothing.

Part of the Tank Farm

At 10.30 in the morning I sent all the staff off the premises and would expect them back at 11.30. Most of them were of similar mind to me and just stood around on the road outside while I stood with my back to the No. 5 tank. It was a matter of intelligence over emotions and although I was feeling nervous, I *knew* there was no bomb. At 11.30 we went back to work and had no more phone calls.

But the damage was done, and Bill and his family were getting pretty depressed by the awful situation. His daughter (being Protestant) had attended a Protestant school, met a Protestant boy who joined the RUC and was shot in the leg. That did it. Bill resigned and headed for Sussex.

1981 and '82 were difficult years commercially. Although the plant started up production on 9 December 1981, we had difficulty in meeting our debts and our cash flow was very tight. As we expanded our business both nationally and internationally, we were not receiving the support from the Bank of Ireland that we needed. The problem was a classical one concerning proof of ownership of stock, a common situation in the oil business. We were purchasing large quantities of contaminated and virgin oils from different sources, from refineries and oceangoing tankers which were mixed together in 30,000-gallon tanks. This required significantly increased working capital, but the Bank of Ireland weren't happy identifying ownership as security for their funds.

This was a feature common to all oil trading and we turned to BNP Paribas, a bank specialising in the oil industry and familiar with such situations. They offered a solution but found it difficult to work with the Bank of Ireland which couldn't handle the problem but didn't want another bank getting part of the cake. However patience and perseverance worked and we were able to keep moving on, building up our turnover over the following few years to nearly Ir£20 million (€45M in 2020). We had confirmed Stokes, Kennedy, Crowley as Auditors in 1981 and appointed Adrian Gallagher and Tom Kirrane as joint Managing Directors while I continued as Chief Operating Officer.

The period from April 1983 through 1984 was one of the busiest of my life.

While I continued to sell fuel oil for Atlas Oil and open up a significant number of large accounts, this did not fill my time and I busied myself widening my areas of interest. My consultancy to the C.I.I. led to many other contacts. I was invited to join the I.D.A. task force for Sligo, and ANCO. I joined Sligo Chamber of Commerce and was made a Director of Sligo Industrial Development Corporation. I lectured on business start up in Monaghan, Portlaoise, Kilkeel, Co. Down, and more. I got to know senior managers in the NBST, Irish Productivity Centre, IMI Innovation Centre, Devco, ESB Consultancy, joined the board of the National Fire Safety Council, worked with CTT, Trinity College Statistical Dept, and UCD Industrial Innovation.

During the next two years the company became more and more profitable. On the industrial fuel side, we became major vendors of heavy fuel oils. We developed small import facilities in Waterford and had leased two small coastal tankers to ship contaminated oils from Milford Haven. We had become national distributors of diesel oil and had appointed a number of authorised agents. We were planning import facilities in Drogheda and Belfast. Profits in 1985 and 1986 were substantial and were expected to grow steadily. It seemed to me that this might be a good time to sell our shares if we could find a suitable buyer.

I had been keeping in touch with 3Is and discussing with some banks the various options open to Helen and I. In January and February 1986 I met AIIB several times, Ulster Investment Bank, and Irish Intercontinental Bank, keeping them all informed on our business growth and profitability.

In August of that year I informed the other directors that we would sell all our shares and that 3Is were interested in financing an MBO, it then became a serious negotiation. How much and when?

I appointed Irish Intercontinental Bank to act for Helen and me while 3Is would keep the other directors' expectations realistic. September and October passed quickly and by November we were close to agreement on the price. As well as the money, the timing was important to us and we wanted the deal to crystallise in the following financial year, i.e. April 1987. The Management appointed William Fry as their solicitor. Gerry Charlton, Paul Keane and IIB worked on a contract of sale to be ready in December for signature in January 1987. Everything was agreed in principle but of course the lawyers had to have their day.

The lawyers in Dublin continued their legal posturing right up to the wire. Paul Keane caught the last plane to London on 14 April (a big birthday for Helen), and we met him at Heathrow airport to sign off on the deal. Paul stayed overnight and flew back to Dublin on the 15th.

I received a welcome call on 14 April from Paul Keane to say that full payment had been received.

Deal done. Time to move on.

INBETWEEN: RETURN TO ATLAS OIL

Forty years later, when we called in, we saw how the IDA support had worked out.

Helen describes the occasion:

> On 21 July, on our way back from a holiday in Killarney, we stopped in Portlaoise and called, uninvited, to the Atlas Oil plant. It had been forty years since we sold it and we were somewhat nervous. We were delighted by the reception we got from Anne Fitzpatrick, who is a director of the company now. She joined in 1989 and knew all about Fred and how the company started in Sligo growing tomatoes as an energy user, development and cash cow. She is hugely proud of the company and loves coming to work every day. She is as proud of it as if it were her own.
>
> Atlas grew from its start in Sligo in 1978 starting with the famous Guy Warrior truck with the twisted chassis which Fred first drove to learn the procedure. We went to Portlaoise in 1980, and the group now sells seventy million litres in ROI, seven million litres in Northern Ireland and sixty million litres in the UK. They now employ seventy people in Portlaoise, three hundred in Ireland and eighteen hundred in total.

The group was split into Emo Oil, now owned by DCC, and Atlas Oil now owned by ENVA – everyone in Portlaoise still calls it Atlas Oil.

The recycled oil mostly goes to Roadstone and tarmacking plants. They built a twenty-million-gallon tank for extra storage during the non-tarmacking period. There are about forty processing and storage tanks there now.

Fred is very chuffed that she knew about the pair of us.

One of our first employees, Eugene Martin, joined us in Sligo in 1975, he retired last year.

Our earliest and most successful employee, Adrian Gallagher, joined us in 1972. He became a shareholder and Managing Director and played a pivotal role in building the company from start-up to integration of corporate investors and overseas expansion. He now heads up Greenway Financial Advisors, a Dublin financial consultancy. Sincere thanks to Adrian, to Anne Fitzpatrick, Eugene Martin and the many others for their support in the success story

CHAPTER 11

THE NATIONAL ENTERPRISE AGENCY

HAVING MET MEL HEALY at the N.B.S.T. in 1983 to discuss a possible Government-funded venture capital programme, we met again in January 1984 to talk about my joining the newly-formed National Enterprise Agency (NEA). It would provide seed capital to deserving projects which carried too much risk for the private sector. After several meetings with Mel and the Chairman of the NEA, Peter Keenan, I was hired as one of a six-person team on a three-day basis, an opportunity which was to prove very fulfilling over the next two and a half years.

I soon became busy in the NEA assessing different investment opportunities and quickly realised the amount of political interference that we would experience. Almost any serious proposal was followed by a call from a TD or a Minister asking for favourable treatment. At a Board presentation, I successfully advised against supporting a national consortium of agricultural machinery manufacturers and ruffled quite a few feathers. Another application for investment was made by a certain Senator who wanted to develop a factory for handling peat. He wouldn't take no for an answer and we had several Ministers leaning on us. We didn't budge.

Soon afterwards Mel asked me to work as a Marketing Director of the newly formed Irish Health Care Development

Corporation (IHSDC). This was an investment that I wouldn't have approved as a suitable commercial investment for a number of reasons. It was an amateur, unplanned venture into a highly professional industry. We were underfunded, understaffed and without even the backing of our own Health Department. I wanted to support Mel so I went on a pre-planned trip to Riyadh and prepared a joint bid with Park Healthcare, a subsidiary of Aer Lingus which was also seeking to diversify. We were not successful.

Networking with other agencies, we sought a JV partner in Saudi Arabia and soon identified the Ali Reza Group, a company whose efforts to work with the ESB consultancy group had fallen through. We met Harry Gibson, the General Manager, a likeable Belfast man and we all hit it off well. Shortly afterwards, we visited Teymour Ali Reza, a charming sophisticated billionaire. He returned the visit to Dublin and a partnership was formed. The Ali Reza group, currently renamed Rezayat Group, is a Saudi company headquartered in Al Khobar. It trades in thirteen countries, employing 16,000. Teymour is a non-executive Director of Shell Transport and Trading Company.

In June I made another trip to Saudi Arabia on an official visit to meet the Saudi Minister for Health. Routed on Aer Lingus through Heathrow, a problem arose when my luggage didn't arrive with me in Heathrow. I was traveling in jeans and didn't relish a formal meeting the following day without a suit. A quick call back to Dublin saw it on the next flight which arrived before my BA flight to Riyadh. So that situation was saved. The following morning, I was in the Ambassadorial car with His Excellency Sean O'Huiginn on our way to meet the Saudi Minister of Health. I confess to feeling proud to be Irish with the two tricolors on the bonnet of the stately limousine.

'Are you sure you know what you want to say at this important international meeting?'

I reassured the Ambassador that I was well-experienced in senior professional presentations. However, I smiled as I thought of the potential situation if I had been wearing jeans.

Later I attended a reception in Teymour's Riyadh home for Barry Desmond, the Irish Minister for Health, the Saudi Minister of Health, the Ambassador and many VIPs.

In October I prepared a bid for a healthcare programme for King Khalid Military City (KKMC) located near Hafr Al Batin, about 350 miles into the desert. In November I spent three weeks in Saudi Arabia and again in December. When we learned that we were short listed for KKMC Seamus Healy, Harry Gibson and I spent four days on site on a fact-finding visit. We met Captain Al Kwai who would play an important role in the next two years. We were to staff and manage a thirty-bed hospital and five clinics including two dental clinics. We would care for the garrison soldiers and their families. We would also look after walk-in patients. These were mostly young, dehydrated Bedouin mothers, about to give birth to the smallest little infants I have ever seen. There were more of them than had been indicated in the Bid documents.

Another surprise was the occasional victim of a high-speed motor accident, usually very seriously injured. These were mostly wealthy sons with top of the range Ferraris, Maserati's and the like driven by men often on a high from food after fasting.

The Saudi military had a challenging bureaucracy and it was typical of them that we would get an almost impossible time for mobilization. It was only on 23 December that we were awarded the contract which was to start on 1 February 1985. This was the first item on the RTE news on 24 December described as a £20 million Christmas present for the IHSDC.

We went into action on 26 December, and with only five weeks to mobilise up to six hundred staff we had a tough challenge. Using HR contractors and hiring extra staff we spent the first three months of the year advertising, interviewing, networking and employing. We had sufficient staff in post to take over the programme on 1 February, but only just.

During our first twenty-four hours we delivered a premature one-kilogram baby for a dehydrated underweight Bedouin woman, and successfully operated on a Thailander who had ruptured his spleen falling off the roof.

My job was to liaise with Capt Al Kwai and Lt Colonel Al Otaishan, Director of Military Works and I found this very difficult as they turned down many of the recommended employees, preferring Muslims. I would not be able to describe the difficulties and frustrations that were a daily occurrence in the hospital in Saudi, so I will just list a few of my memories.

The bisexual Sergeant Yahya was a constant source of challenge due to his sexual proclivity. The security wall around the Philippine nurses was only about four feet tall and the Saudi soldiers were an ongoing threat to the girls, especially the sergeant. I got some control over his activities by persuading Captain Al Kwai to make the Sergeant the NCO in charge of security over my nurses. This meant that he was directly responsible to the Captain and in the firing line if the nurses were molested. Things improved considerably after that.

We were running a thirty-bed hospital which was adequate for the needs of the small city, but there was a gleaming new six hundred-bed hospital mothballed just across the road. It had every possible medical facility including two CAT scanners at a time when there was only one in all of Ireland. Years later, we realised the rationale for this hospital during the first Gulf war, when KKMC became the hub for Stormin' Norman's thrust into Kuwait up its western border rather than attacking from the sea as the Iraqis had expected. What long-range planning to establish this huge medical facility so many years ahead!

A happy memory: we had only two baby incubators, but there were lots in the new hospital over the road. When we needed to incubate seven tiny babies it was useless asking Al Kwai for support, so in the middle of the night the Irish team broke into the hospital and borrowed a number of incubators. I invited the General to visit our nursery and he loved the little babies. No questions were ever asked.

On another occasion, we observed that everything that didn't move was being painted. Something was up but what? One day we were ordered to have a full medical team standing by as the King would visit tomorrow for a short stay. None of the royal party needed our care, but a problem arose when one of the king's horses suffered a simple cut to his leg and we were asked to treat it. Our Orthopaedic Surgeon refused to work on an animal and a difficult situation could have arisen. However, our Chief of Medicine Pat O'Neill did the job and all was well. A little while later Pat received a present of a gorgeous leather briefcase with gold trimmings and the royal crest on the cover.

Dealing with the army could be frustrating. Occasionally, when a multiple high-speed crash on the motorway brought a fleet of ambulances into our A&E, the melée of paramedics, and nursing staff was complicated by a proliferation of seemingly superfluous soldiers. When I tried to act like the boss and bring about some order I was ignored and gestured to leave it to the army.

Another day, I was talking with a doctor in a corridor when he leaned against a fire button causing it to alarm. Trying to reassure staff members that it wasn't a fire, I was ignored. The trained staff followed their training. I was semi-lifted out of the building still protesting and only allowed in when the all-clear had been given.

———————◆◆◆———————

We won one battle which I recall with pleasure. Colonel Al Otaishan had announced his intention of a formal inspection of the hospital. I met him and after my welcome, he swept through our corridors with all his authority which was fine and to be expected.

The Colonel was about six foot two inches and wearing heavy army boots. Escorted by about four large officers, they looked like the March of the Elephants in *Jungle Book*, left-right, left-right as he approached the Operating Theaters. Suddenly a shrill STOP brought them to a shuddering halt. The Senior Operating Theater Nurse was formidable. 'This is a sterile area!' Maggie, our diminutive Dublin Head Nurse, was in charge. 'No one allowed in here without scrubs.'

The effect was theatrical. All the pomp evaporated. The group gently retreated with muttered apologies and slightly embarrassed smiles. A nice incident, which showed off our hospital discipline, satisfied the army's requirements, and put a smile on my face.

In May of that year I was appointed to the board of the IHSDC and persuaded to take the job of General Manager of IHSDC and of the joint venture. That meant that I would work from Dublin, reporting to the Board, and marketing the campaign, but with a hands on responsibility for the operational side. Shortly afterwards I received an urgent call when our anaesthetist, allegedly, caused the death of a young Thai who was being operated on for a broken wrist. By the time I arrived, the local management had sent her out of the country en route to Dublin.

I had to take the heat. We conducted an enquiry and sought to lower the tension referring to the will of Allah. It was a difficult, confrontational meeting. Colonel Al Otaishan was furious that the culprit had left the country. As someone had to pay, it would have to be me as head of the operation. I was able to point out that the Irish Minister for Health was the ultimate head of the operation, and would I ask the Ambassador to require the Minister to take the blow. The Colonel backed down. Phew!

Our partner, Teymour Ali Reza, had homes in many countries, one in Mayfair with an indoor swimming pool, located next door to a similar one owned by his father who usually lived in Houston where Teymour also had a home. His main residence was in Riyadh, but Harry Gisson brought me to see a house he also kept in Dhahran. In this huge unoccupied house I saw an antique Japanese ornament which the Japanese had given to Teymour on one of his visits.

In August 1985, the Directors of the NEA/IHSDC were invited for dinner and a meeting in his beautiful Geneva residence in the hills overlooking Lake Leman. Our son Peter was working in the Hilton Hotel, Geneva, so Helen came with me on a private visit. When Harry told Teymour that Helen was in town, he invited her to join the official party for dinner; a memorable evening in many ways.

In November Harry O'Sullivan, now chairman of the IHSDC announced his intention to visit KKMC and I accompanied him. When we landed at Riyadh airport there was a real problem. Harry couldn't enter the country because his passport was locked away in his suitcase which had gone through to the terminal. Being familiar with Saudi bureaucracy it seemed an impossible situation, but I managed it by creating a big fuss about the Chairman not being allowed entry, making it the fault of the immigration staff. They allowed me to enter immigration, identify his case open it up and go back through immigration with his passport. I kept a close eye on him for the rest of the trip until I saw him on to a plane for London.

During the next six months, I was busy networking around the medical world trying to persuade doctors to work for us in SA. As part of this task I had planned a visit to Scandinavia where my Board thought we might have some success. Although it was winter, we badly needed doctors and specialists and I was hoping to drum up interest. Helen met me at Heathrow as I arrived from Riyadh and together we visited Oslo, Stockholm, Uppsala and Helsinki. Helen travelled at our personal cost. I visited medical associations in each country and made my case promoting KKMC as a great opportunity. Returning to Ireland we bid for another contract in SA. In addition, I was also studying franchising for the NEA as a means of developing business and creating jobs.

I began 1986 meeting Lloyd's of London Members Agents. I was interested in becoming a name, but needed to know more and was trying to identify a good agent.

In April I made my last visit to Saudi Arabia. I was running out of enthusiasm for the IHSDC concept and felt that I had nothing more to contribute. Seeking tax advice, Helen and I had an interesting investigative trip to Andorra, Monaco and San Marino in June, and upon my return I resigned from the NEA.

I had joined Dublin Rotary Club and was enjoying the lively social side of the club. I was busy consulting a taxation expert in Stokes Kennedy Crowley and planning our move to England.

Helen had a hysterectomy in September and was well treated in Holles St. Hospital. She behaved herself, keeping quiet and letting her body heal. I was glad to be able to mind her. During December I met a number of franchisors in the UK seeking ideas for starting a new business. I wasn't prepared to retire yet.

We were moving on.

CHAPTER 12

LLOYD'S OF LONDON

UBERRIMA FIDES – UTMOST GOOD FAITH

THE PURPORTED ATTRACTION OF membership of Lloyd's was its long tradition of *Uberrima Fides*, utmost good faith between the main players, the risk-taking bookies called underwriters and the Member's Agents, representing the 'names' which is what we, the investors, were called. In fact, the representation of 'utmost good faith' was a façade hiding one of the biggest confidence scams in the risqué gambling game played by Lloyd's.

Sometime previously, my friend Joe Flood advised me "You are able to handle the sharks of Dublin, but the sharks in London are much bigger." Looking back, it should have been obvious that Lloyd's longtime marine pool would be well populated by sharks.

I believe my decision to join Lloyd's was a good one in pure business terms, selling insurance risk. Anyone in business is taking a risk and shouldn't be there if uncomfortable with risk. But it must be a measured risk based on full disclosure. This was to be expected as a given in an august association which for hundreds of years has protected its standard of *uberrima fides*, utmost good faith between the underwriter and the broker and in turn the names.

With son Peter at Lloyd's in London, CEO Mercanto, A I marketing

The proposition was to make a profit in the good years and take a hit on bad ones. If we had had a few years of profitable trading to build up a buffer of profit this would create an acceptable risk scenario, provided everyone was telling the truth. What I didn't anticipate was a large section of the membership at all levels including the chairman were prepared to simply lie. They either understated their liabilities or, using insider knowledge, reduced their risk by reinsuring their long tail exposures to uninformed syndicates – sacrificial lambs if you like – such as the Outhwaite syndicate.

We believed that our choice of Member's Agent was critical; firstly, did they have the knowledge, the contacts and the clout to secure access to good syndicates? Helen and I interviewed eight Member Agents and selected the John Donner agency. John, a third-generation old hand, explained to us how the market works. Each trading period was for a single year, but the books weren't closed at year-end as another two years were allowed for all outstanding claims to be settled, making it a three year cycle. Thus, it was possible to suffer severe liabilities in, for example, 1988 and not realize it until 1991.

They explained the different types of syndicates and the sectors in which they specialized. Some syndicates were 'long-tailed' and some 'short-tailed'. The 'short-tailed' were newer syndicates or ones that specialize in motor and aviation, where losses were quickly accounted for and fully paid inside the three years and no long-term liabilities. 'Long-tailed' were syndicates with long term disputed or unrealized losses in areas such as asbestosis, pollution and ecological claims, public liability and similar. Such syndicates had adopted another method of trading. At the end of each three-year cycle, if it couldn't or hadn't settled all the ongoing liabilities, they would park them together with a large sum of money which was hopefully estimated to be sufficient for the future. They would then declare a result either positive or negative on the risks that could be closed off. As a consequence, there frequently were syndicates reporting a profit and large bonuses and commissions for staff while storing up reserves and liabilities for the future. We were told that long tails were good business because they had very large cash assets earning enough interest to produce good results and sufficient to see of any old risks. But were they large enough?

The reality was, there was a lot of wishful thinking in the room. Any well-informed old hand knew that the long-tail reserves were grossly inadequate for the asbestosis claims clearly mushrooming in the US courts. A further complication of 'long tails' was the further delay of liabilities through the purchase of a specialist RITC policy to further postpone claims. This was yet another means of hiding the actual liability by passing the buck, paying for Reinsurance To Close and pushing liability further down the track for future names to pay.

But there was a worse nightmare maturing in the form of claims for damages caused by pollution. For decades, thousands of American chemical companies had treated the virgin countryside as a waste dump, causing toxic effects in countless situations. This first evidenced in the early 1970s, when Shells Rocky Mountain Arsenal practice of dumping poisonous waste was publicized. It was soon followed by a growing number of pollution claims monitored by the US EPA, the Office of Technology, the Chemical Manufacturers Association. As the public outcry grew Federal Agencies became involved and legislation was introduced by Presidents Carter and Reagan. Various reports indicated great numbers of polluted sites, estimated at 10,000 or more, potential cost of many billions merging into trillions. When the legal profession realized the bonanza waiting for them, lawyers in their thousands swarmed onto the scene pushing claims. Many claims were not valid, but thousands of lawyers had their field-day as they fought American and Lloyd's lawyers in US courts. Indeed, the US lawyers may have made more money than the claimants.

The flood started in 1980 when Shell sued Lloyd's for nearly two billion dollars. When I applied for membership this was never mentioned. Additionally, thousands of asbestosis claims were in Lloyd's as far back as the 1970s, with forecasts of claims arising from an estimated 200,000 related deaths.

At first, I thought that John Donner was a good choice, but he had considerable knowledge of what was coming down the track and he didn't share it with us. In fact, he put us on long-tail syndicates with all their baggage.

A significant number of insiders knew what was looming. What to do? They produced a clever innovative idea; wait for a couple of good years showing excellent results, then reduce the capital amount required for acceptance as a member, publicize recent profits and attract in a lot more members. Increase membership to such a size that the old liabilities would be dwarfed by the increased cash flow. Membership grew in the 1980s from 6,000 to 32,000. Known as 'recruit to dilute', it could well have been called 'sheep-in for clipping'. I was one of those sheep, but it was on the basis of the biggest scam in the three hundred-year history of Lloyd's trading. It was a total revocation of its long-vaunted claim of utmost good faith.

Syndicates now had many more funds to play with, so they got greedy. The principle of prudent insurance management is to take a leading role on say, the first 10% of the risk and pass the other 90% outside Lloyd's and around the world's insurance markets. This would limit the name's exposure to a bad claim. Many smartassed dealers brought some of the risk back into Lloyd's, giving them more bites at the cherry and more commission each time. Their syndicates sometimes finished upholding 25%/30% of the risk, quite contrary to insurance prudent practice. When a claim developed, the cash required to settle would travel around the world then back into Lloyd's to hit the members again and again. This became known as the 'spiral'. The result was that that senior members of the syndicates could earn millions in commission while their syndicates lost money and bled their names nearly dry.

We were informed that catastrophes could be expected about every four or more years, and that they were good for business. They frightened bit players out of the market, drove up rates which would pay for the claims and ensure increased profit the following year.

Sounded good but it didn't work that way for us. Had we been members throughout the 1980s we could have built up sufficient reserves to withstand an occasional catastrophe. We joined in 1988, just in time for five catastrophes over the following twenty-four months. In 1988, Piper Alpha oil rig blew up in the North Sea, Hurricane Gilbert wiped out Jamaica, in 1989 the Exxon Valdez was followed by the San Francisco earthquake, and the Phillips Petroleum plant explosion. Hurricane Hugo hit Charleston in September and became the second costliest catastrophe to that time. Also, asbestosis claims surfaced in a big way.

The final account for 1988 revealed a loss of £500 million, the first loss in two decades. Things worsened as the claims spiraled around the room. During the following five years Lloyd racked up losses totaling £7.9 billion from 1988 to 1992. We lost a lot of money. It was painful, with a number of suicides. Thousands of names resigned, but we held our nerve and stayed in for some more years clawing back some profit on the basis of reduced capacity and better rates. In 1994 an in-house reinsurer Equitas took on all my liabilities up to 1993 for a one-off payment. In 1996 annual accounting was adopted.

In 1996 Lloyd's offered its members a reconstruction and renewal deal which would close off much of our risk. This was accepted by 95% of the members including me and we started to sleep nights. I resigned in 1998 and by 2001 was able to move on and close a most unfortunate chapter.

I leave the last word to John Donner: 'I have never used the word conspiracy, but what I do say is that information which was privy to a handful of people at the very top of Lloyd's was not property disseminated.' In fact, the Deputy Chairman had urged Members Agents back in 1982 to inform potential new members the facts about asbestosis and the manner in which their syndicates' liabilities had been covered. Had Donner advised me of all the risks inherent in long tail syndicates I would not have joined.

CHAPTER 13

GREENMAN, THE BIG VENTURE

RESILIENCE, THE BACKBONE OF AN ENTREPRENEUR

'THERE WILL BE NO hurricane, only strong winds,' Michael Fish famously assured the nation on the evening of 15 October, 1987, 'worries about a possible hurricane were unfounded.' The British Met Office had been tracking a tropical depression crossing the Atlantic and had decided that it would only have a slight effect on England. BBC forecaster Fish would never live down the misinformation. I had looked at the barometer on my way to bed. The pointer had dropped to the extreme bottom of the dial, something I had never seen before, so I concluded that it was broken. It wasn't.

For the next seven hours Helen and I slept through the worst storm since 1703, winds of 95–110 mph wreaking enormous damage and many deaths. It was a night of terror, caravans flying through the air, roofs flicked away like frisbees, cars flattened beneath trees. Downed power lines draped the countryside in high voltage chaos. A ferry had been driven aground at Folkestone, London Underground and railways skidded to a halt, and commuters were told to stay at home. Gatwick Airport, the Bank of England and the Stock Market were all in darkness. Eighteen people were dead. The insurance claims would top £500 million.

We escaped relatively unscathed. Eight trees were blown down, one on a shed which we subsequently replaced with a tennis pavilion, courtesy of an agreeable insurance company.

'Hello, anyone home?' It was a neighbour, James Aarvold, on his way to work. His usual way was completely blocked by fallen trees so he came through our garden. With no electricity he wasn't yet aware that the storm had disrupted power and communications to the extent that the London Stock Exchange wouldn't open.

At that time the market was overpriced, and a number of brokers were anxious to reduce their holdings in London on the Friday. With the market closed the pressure to sell built up over the weekend, so when the New York market opened on what became known as Black Monday, there was a rush to sell. However, buyers were cagey and reluctant to buy so that the market didn't function. Prices fell sharply, the market got confused and some systems couldn't cope.

The NYSE was reeling from a drop of 140 points until the market crashed at 9:30 a.m. World markets fed off each other's panic through the week, hitting a loss of 23% mid-week and a final loss of 35% before corrections began.

They say that a fool and his money are easily parted, and I was proving this to be true.

We had recently placed a large part of our funds in the market, managed by brokers Rothschilds and Sons. We lost a great deal of money. Added to this was the hit we took while I was a name at Lloyd's of London. We had invested heavily in a Tenerife holiday homes development under construction by the builder who had the best reputation on the island, until they called in the receiver.

It had taken us a quarter of a century of hard work to save a comfortable pension and only two years to lose half of it. It was time to go back to work.

Seeking to prove that the Atlas Oil success wasn't down to luck, circumstances had contrived to make me do it all again and I would.

Only this time, bigger.

The most difficult time in an entrepreneur's life is when they can't find a project. It's not possible to identify the right opportunity if it isn't there. A golden rule in my book was not to commit to any project if it wasn't absolutely right for me. This was no exception. Lacking my own ideas, I explored a number of franchises: Confetti, Snappy Snaps, catering franchises and many more but none were right for me.

Finally, one day when I was really getting frustrated, I happened on an opportunity. In my accountant's office I notice an object on the floor beside a waste bin. It looked like a small radio and was on its way to the disposal chute. It was a laser cartridge, a recent invention by Hewlett-Packard for use in a high-quality printer. Laser cartridges were filled with toner powder instead of ink and were being replaced when empty. A new industry was emerging to refill them. It could be a win-win business, offering significant savings to the customers and excellent profit margin to recyclers. A new idea, little was known about the 'How To'. It took Helen and I over a year to research and learn the basic technology and sources of material supplies. There were some snake oil versions around, but we avoided these and in 1991 we trained in Seattle and Austin, Texas. It was great to be back at work.

There were over a hundred components in a cartridge, mostly nuts, bolts, screws and wires, only four or five items that required replacement. The toner powder was finely ground carbon material containing certain additives and it was important to find a quality supplier. We called our process 'remanufacturing' because it required complete disassembly and cleaning of the cartridge. This was a high precision job conducted under negative atmosphere with Hepa filtration. Helen was our first technician and typically improved our processes. She then trained our first two technicians while I trained two telesales staff.

I had envisioned a modest operation, one to give us a small income while our investments grew. Little did I anticipate that we would expand this business into a significant international group of five factories and three warehouses in England, Spain and Bulgaria and a distribution warehouse in Maastricht, Holland, employing over three hundred in four countries. It kept me busy for nearly twenty years and gave us an income to live in considerable comfort, to support our children in boarding schools, universities and their weddings.

It would have been unwise to commit to leasing a factory at start up. We converted one bedroom into our 'factory' and started production. Trading as Access Lasercall, I soon realized the positive implications of recycling, and changed the name to Greenman Toners Limited which over time grew into a group. We started in January 1992 and after six months sales had reached two hundred cartridges per month and climbing. We moved into a thousand square foot unit in Epsom which we soon mezzanined into two thousand square feet. By 1995 we were recycling 45,000 cartridges and had good cash flow which prompted the move into a 10,000 square foot factory, also in Epsom.

That year everything was going well when we had a sudden unexpected problem. I had a blocked artery, which caused a minor heart attack. It was time to employ a managing director to relieve me. Aiming for early recovery, I focused on rehab programs and by the spring of 1996 I was back at work as Chairman. I really enjoyed the strategic challenges of growing into a medium-sized manufacturing and marketing group led by a growing structure of management.

It was especially a joy to employ so many happy people and it was natural for me to adopt a paternalistic attitude to them and to take a strong line if anyone mistreated them. Away from my hearing, they referred to me as the 'Old Man'. One group of employees from Sri Lanka were reliable workers and studiously punctual. While I knew that they came to work by car, it was sometime before I learned that nine of them traveled in one car, six in the car and three hunkered down in the boot.

A particular cause for satisfaction was the growth of a management team of which I was truly proud. They were recruited in various ways. The capable Production Director, Robert Bishop, was recommended to me in a personal call from a competitor who would have employed him except for distance. Rob was a star. The Sales Director, Mark Dawson, another star, was headhunted by me. I had met and assessed him on a number of occasions and brought my MD to Holland to interview him. I agreed that Mark would get the same equity as Rob Bishop.

We learned that a supply of empty toner cartridges was the essential lifeblood of our production and we soon became adept in this area. Running into a surplus of empties created the opportunity to sell these to other recyclers with the results that trading in empty cartridges soon became an important part of our work. To administer this section of the business we had recruited a junior office administrator who performed so unusually well that I realized we had hired real talent. Paul Freshwater took over the empties division and grew it into a subsidiary company, K2 Ltd. In 2001, needing more space, it moved into an additional 20,000 square foot warehouse in Camberly, Hampshire. By now, it was shipping forty-foot containers of empties to the USA and to China.

We obtained a contract from Samsung to recycle under their label, having signed a contract with Paul Choi from Korea. We opened a distribution centre in Maastricht which was effective in supporting our considerable sales in Europe

In 2002 I was surprised when the three directors approached me in a group and asked for a meeting. They had a problem. Their joint message was that they wanted me to resume control as Chief Executive and let our managing director go. They felt the group had no longer a vision and had lost its buzz. This was rather flattering to my ego but it required rough justice on my MD and more early mornings for me.

An expanding business always produces challenges and we had a growing demand for more empties from K2. We turned to France seeking further supplies and suitable premises. Mistakenly, we approached at official level and got sucked into a bureaucracy who entertained us to a number of fine French lunches in small villages desperate for work but with no modern factory buildings available. Repeatedly, we were shown obsolete steel mills and vast warehouses while our time and costs mounted.

Finally, in November I found a bright modern factory building that met our specifications. Located in Longwy near the Luxemburg border, the owner and I agreed on a most agreeable deal of rent and an option to buy at a price fixed for three years. We were looking good until we enquired about planning permission and were shocked to learn that this process would require five different stages of approval and could take up to a year or more. We felt rather let down and left France in disgust.

I then turned to Barcelona where we kept our approach private and were greatly assisted by the local Anglo-Spanish Chamber of Commerce.

We soon became established in an industrial unit just South of Barcelona. Our HR Manager organized recruitment and staffing of the unit, I went over to interview personnel for the position of General Manager and appointed Jose Molero. Paul

Freshwater promoted the business and things were going well at K2 when an unexpected tragedy ruined everything.

Senora Molero, Jose's wife, was murdered.

Having parked her car in the underground carpark below their apartment block, she was innocently unloading her shopping when she was shot dead. I have no knowledge of motive or perpetrator, but we and the Spanish were distraught. I spent the next two days in Barcelona supporting Jose and all the staff, but the damage was done. The heart had been totally knocked out of the business and it never recovered. We closed the plant in late 2004.

The pricing in our market had become extremely competitive as supplies arrived from Eastern Europe and third world countries. Several of our largest competitors had switched some of their production to Eastern Europe and Southeast Asia. We knew it was time to do the same and on 1 August I made my first approach to the Indian authorities.

It was to prove a fruitless exercise. During the next eight weeks we wrote, faxed and emailed the development agencies in northwest India and received almost no response or interest. I was feeling quite frustrated when we learned that the cost of production in Bulgaria was lower than that of India.

My inquiries into the Embassy and Chamber of Commerce in Bulgaria soon gave us details of wages and conditions. Over the next two months I made useful contacts in Sofia and learned that it was a low-cost country with stable government and currency. It had a legacy of post-Communist practices but was due to join the EU in 2006. It promised a suitable and safe location for low cost production.

In a fast-moving business, things are never static. I had put in another five years of general management and at seventy-two, the Board and I thought it time to seek a younger CEO, who would take the top job and lead us into the next phase of our business.

Board member Michael Higgins led the procedure, using a headhunting agency to find us the right man. The Board approved the selection of Malcolm Hughes, a sophisticated Scouser and a Liverpool football supporter. He quickly got up to speed which left me time to focus on our next major diversion, Bulgaria. 2005 was going to be an exciting year.

CHAPTER 14
BULGARIA

THE TWO MEN WERE clearly carrying. They had exited the third car in the fleet of long bodied black Mercs with darkened windows and were gesturing to us to get in the middle vehicle. I looked at Rob Bishop, my Production Director and thought, 'What are we doing here?'

We had only visited Bulgaria twice, but we had learned that carrying firearms was quite legal, provided one had a license, readily available to ex-army and police personnel. An armed chauffeur/guard/PA could be hired 24/7 for about €200 per month and we saw many of them accompanying their bosses on the way to meetings in the international hotels. We understand that the illegal mafia controlled much of the economy and we were about to meet one of them.

We were there because our Austrian bank manager, in seeking to help us find a suitable factory premises had arranged for us to meet a 'Property Developer'.

Our first two visits to Bulgaria had been challenging. It was approaching winter and very cold. Seeking suitable factory premises, we met government officials who showed us a variety of old communist era buildings, big and ugly, some in flatted factories. They had been stripped of every fitting, even windows and roof tiles right down to concrete skeletons and were totally unsuitable. We were glad of some advice from our banks and we were going to find out how Bulgaria works.

We decided to stand our ground at the Radisson Grand Hotel and let the property developer show his face. He was a normal enough man unlike the minders who with slicked back hair, wrapped around sunglasses and both carrying a gun, looked like the Blues Brothers. We got in a Merc and were brought to the industrial city of Pernic, just twenty kilometers southwest of Sofia. He showed us around a large site of old derelict communist factories. When I pointed out that these were totally unsuitable for us he promised to refurbish our choice of factory with good access etc, entirely rent-free if we could help him out. Apparently, he had secured this potentially valuable property free of charge from the State, provided he created employment for a certain number of jobs – which he was failing to do. He wanted to borrow our employees and present them to the state as his own. All one hundred employees would appear on his books and he would pay them while we paid him. A total scam. I took care to appear interested, would put it to my board and call him. I was glad to get away from him and his minders.

On the last day of our third visit – just when we were really desperate – we found a concrete shell which could be made functional. It was on the grounds of a golf course in the village of Ichtiman, a town of 20,000 people located thirty kilometres east of Sofia just off the motorway to Plovdiv. The buildings were owned by Air Sofia and had adequate office space for administration staff and two thousand square feet of factory space, large enough for a startup. There were two other buildings nearby which we could convert. In seeking to acquire the premises it was necessary to go through the bureaucratic tendering procedures required by Bulgarian law. Our tender was accepted, and we acquired our site in August 2005.

On our first visits to Ichtiman I noticed groups of dark-featured men, women and children hanging around the streets. They looked down-and-out with jet black hair and darker skins – not a good-looking people. I learned that these were Romas, an ethnic minority of 5-10% of Bulgaria's population. Over 80% of them were living below the poverty line so it wasn't surprising that they looked unkempt.

When I advertised for a Works Manager, we had four applicants but one stood out. A female, she had adequate English and two degrees in Business Administration and Engineering. Her father had wanted a boy but when his daughter was born and growing up he introduced her to engines rather than dolls and she grew up both a practical and qualified engineer. She was an ideal person for her position. Her English improved quickly as we got to know each other better and I introduced her to the many idioms that permeate the language.

When we started to recruit other staff we soon learned that other Bulgarians didn't want to work alongside Romas. Thinking of my experience of the religious divide in Northern Ireland, I decided that up to 50% workforce would be made up of Romas, provided that their performance was up to our standard. After a little friction this was accepted and we soon found that the Romas worked harder than the others –they were so glad to be treated as equals and to have a job. We learned that other employers paid workers 60% officially and 40% under the table to save taxes. This suited both parties until an employee lost the job or became ill and suffered a poor unemployment benefit. This wasn't for us. We paid more than other employers and deducted the appropriate taxes.

Bulgaria was very poor. A dead cow on the roadside in the town centre was not unusual. Worse still, the dead victim of a road accident was seen lying uncovered by the side of the highway. The police were often left at month's end without wages because the municipality had run out of cash. No wonder they sought to penalize motorists, charging spot fines to supplement their incomes. On one occasion we phoned the police to help us handle a problem. When they didn't show we went to the station to discover they had no petrol in their police car.

We found the workforce in Ichtiman extremely dedicated to their jobs and welcomed training . Importantly there was no animosity between the Bulgarians and Romas. I and my management team took care to foster a relaxed atmosphere for our workforce to enjoy their work. The result was a good-humored mood on the shop-floor. We were happy as productivity levels passed our targets. Much of our work had been transferred to Ichtiman, now our main production hub. We had expanded into the second factory some months previously and were to occupy the third unit in the new year.

One day, a male Roma employee arrived at work carrying a big bag of sweets which he distributed to everyone. I was on one of my visits at the time. 'What are you celebrating?' He explained that he and his wife had been trying for a baby for years without success but since he got this good job his wife had become pregnant and had just delivered a healthy baby boy. The father had named him 'Greenman' after the company. A high point in his life, and in mine.

I visited Ichtiman twice that December advising on projects with our works manager and while there I assisted Paul Freshwater, who was appointing an executive to run the collection program for K2.

He would have a week's training in England in the new year

When I first heard about the flood I didn't really understand the extent and the full implications. Our factories had been seriously flooded due to the breach of two separate dams in two different mountain ranges, one in the Balkan Mountain range to the North, the other in the Mila Mountains in the South.

Due to private ownership they were badly maintained and unfit for purpose. Unable to contain the down-pour from a night of violent storms, they both burst, sending hundreds of millions of gallons of water across the entire central plain and flooding our factories to a depth of nine feet.

The force of the flood had burst open doors and damaged specially designed fittings. Boilers and power generators were destroyed. Our stores and finished goods were a write-off; canteen and toilets unusable. A foul smell pervaded our factories which looked like graveyards, our pristine production lines covered in thick layers of mud and debris. The flood had also created a mini lake in a hollow close by.

Our staff worked night and day to restart production and save their jobs while we persuaded our customers that we would restart in a week or so.

We were just getting back into production a week later when unbelievably we were flooded again to a depths of eight feet. This time the flood was due to the Bulgarian Army seeking to clear the mini lake which was a public hazard. They blasted a relief passage to run off the lake into a nearby stream but got it desperately wrong and routed it into our premises.

The staff had worked night and day and had cleared the effects of the first flood but they were exhausted and disheartened. It took weeks to repair the damage and try to produce quality products. But our customers had enough and had gone away. Cash flow had evaporated and most of Greenman resources had been destroyed by Bulgarian floods. Greenman never recovered but K2 wasn't affected.

It was trading well and we later sold it to an American company.

The year was 2007. The company had been another success since 1990. I was seventy-four, and it was certainly time for me to retire. Or was it …?

CHAPTER 15
THE ADVENTURE CONTINUES

The previous twenty years had seen the most adventure and fun in our lives. With short trips to Europe, the longer ones were the more exciting; snorkeling with seals in the Galapagos, ballooning in Namibia, elephant hunting in Rajasthan, meeting Karma Pa, second disciple to the Dalai Lama in McCloud-Ganj, Himalayas (his first is in gaol in China), hunting with lions in Botswana, scuba diving in Mozambique, South Africa, Australia, Turkey, Egypt, Syria, Morocco, Jordan, Scandinavia, Arctic Circle, Ethiopia, Hong Kong, Peru, Ecuador. As I look back, I wonder how I got any work done.

Sleeping quarters in a beehive hut in Swaziland

In recording my stories from the past, I have often referred to Helen's courage through fifty years of exciting living. She was always at my side, no matter what venture I proposed. However, I never fully realized that I was married to an adventurer until one summer's evening in 2006.

Transport in Egypt

Helen and I were dressed as pirates, enjoying a maritime costume party for an ex-Navy friend, when I noticed her in earnest conversation with another lady. When I joined them, they conspicuously changed the subject and it was sometime before I learned what they had been discussing. Helen had been researching details of a skydive and parachute jump and intended to do one to celebrate her seventieth birthday. Did I mind?

Admittedly she had a history of adventurous pursuits; it was Helen who insisted on the scary balloon ride over the sand dunes in Namibia. It was Helen who jumped into a small seaplane we happened on in New England. It was Helen who wanted the helicopter ride into the Grand Canyon and who insisted on draping snakes around her neck in India. This was a lady who, accompanied only by a Mahout guide, rode an elephant into the Indian jungle searching for tigers, a lady who canoed down whitewater rapids to avoid a family of curious hippopotami.

Helen in Berlin to knock down the Wall

OK, but this was different. She was now going to jump out of a plane at 12,000 feet attached to a minder who would guide her hopefully to earth. I was on the ground and at 12,000 feet the plane appeared so small that I could hardly see it, until the jump sergeant pointed it out to me. When the parachutists jumped out of the plane, they looked the size of a pinhead. Scary! Some lady! The jump, took place on 4 April 2007.

Helen marking her 70th birthday

When we had retired back to Ireland, I felt safer, but I was wrong. As 2012 and another signature age approached (seventy-five) I heard her discussing a fund-raising event by abseiling down the side of the tallest building in Limerick. That didn't happen but was replaced by abseiling from the top of the Aviva Stadium in Dublin: an altitude of 156 feet.

The years passed and as 2017 (eighty) approached I heard her talking with my son Michael about a double jump. It was time for a diversion. How would a trip along the Silk Road via Uzbekistan sound? It worked. The jumping out of planes was over, I think.

Daughter Suzanne, author of 12 books

Son Michael, produces TV adverts

Then there was a new challenge: this time, it was me.

It all started when my children asked me to record my many stories for them, which I have now revised in this narrative. As I recalled the excitement of meeting and winning the many challenges in this story, it struck a nascent chord, activating what the economist Schumpeter called 'the spirit of enterprise.' It further brought me back to an adage I coined long ago:

'When you have lived your dreams
you cannot go back to sleeping.'

The whole family

I recalled how much I have learned from twelve challenging situations, from four successful business startups, the experience and know-how I had assimilated. I realized it would be a loss to allow all this knowledge to waste away if I could help some others on their journey towards entrepreneurship.

My book on the subject, *Do You Want to be an Entrepreneur?* will be published later this year and will address many of the issues in starting up a business. It will be a very practical 'how-to', from concept to cashflow. It should prove useful to would-be entrepreneurs.

You might say that the old entrepreneur is at it again.

THIS SPELL BINDING BIOGRAPHY tells of an entrepreneur's determination and success against a remarkable series of unwarranted setbacks, life threatening dangers and competitor spying.

Read how Duffy made a small fortune, only to lose it, then rebuild it bigger and better in a style that could serve as a textbook for successful startups. With an enthusiasm that shines through the entire narrative we follow him and wife Helen as they surmount repeated obstacles, powering on to further adventures. We also travel the world with them, water skiing, scuba diving, parachute-jumping in a hugely enjoyable life.

Aged 87 and disinclined to retire, Duffy, now an author, has written a sister book to this one.

Want to be an Entrepreneur? offers guidance on business startups to aspiring entrepreneurs together with practical tips from his four successful ventures.

Later this year he will publish the biographies of John D Rockefeller and Calouste Gulbenkian 'Two Giants who shaped our oil world'. He has at least two more books in the offing .

Duffy's new career surely warrants the adage. 'Old entrepreneurs never die, they only fade away'.

Printed in Great Britain
by Amazon

77641867R00130